THE

PHOENIX LIBRARY

*

EIGHTEENTH CENTURY
POETRY

*A list
of other titles in the Phoenix Library
will be found at the end
of this book*

EIGHTEENTH CENTURY POETRY

AN ANTHOLOGY CHOSEN

By

W. J. TURNER

CHATTO AND WINDUS
LONDON

First issued in the Phoenix Library
First published 1931

PREFACE

THE eighteenth century has a curious reputation. It is considered materialistic, cold, witty and mannered. Like most reputations, this is based more on what is apparent and superficial than on what is hidden and profound ; yet, nevertheless, it is not wholly false, as a comparison of its poetry with that of the preceding or succeeding centuries will show. It is a fact that some of the greatest minds and imaginations in English history were active during the eighteenth century and are represented here. The intellectual life of England is necessarily involved with that of the rest of Europe, and the eighteenth century was rich in creative genius there also. But perhaps this genius was inclined to take a philosophic and scientific cast ? A highly cultured intellectual society existed, and it was cosmopolitan. The world was small enough. The East and the West hardly existed, and Europe intellectually had one homogeneous society. This society was strong enough to impose its character on youthful talent. So, we shall find in this book (in startling contrast to any anthology of the sixteenth or seventeenth centuries !), not a single true love-song until we come to Robert Burns who, be it noticed, was a peasant, and a man, therefore, free of the conventions of traditional society.

We cannot conclude that for a hundred years men, men of creative fire, lived without passion, therefore we must assume that a certain kind of expression was not in the mode. The fear of making oneself ridiculous is always strong in a new and rich society, and it must be remembered that the eighteenth century in England was the first in which Society in the modern sense existed. In Congreve's *Way of the World*, in the famous scene between Mrs. Millamant and her future husband, we have the attitude of the time perfectly expressed. The lovers promise always to appear in public cold and distant to one another, and even to carry this behaviour as far as possible into their privacy. ' Wit ' and cynicism were artificial flowers, and as such were enormously admired and fanatically cherished because a philosophy which had grown sceptical about nature was ready at hand to believe in them. Man must believe in something.

That is one part of the picture. Alongside these phenomena were others. George Berkeley, for example, who is represented here by a single but significant poem. Berkeley is undoubtedly the acutest and profoundest philosophical thinker the English race has so far produced.[1] In the *Analyst* he criticized Newton's theory of fluxions in a way that has caused him to be hailed by modern mathematicians as a pioneer. Berkeley is the greatest opponent of that scientific materialism which is thought characteristic of the eighteenth century but which is not confined to any age. Much that seems new and mysterious in the thought of modern mathematical physicists may be found in Berkeley, together with a great deal more

[1] Berkeley (later in his life Bishop of Cloyne) was a man of such attractive character that even Pope wrote a tribute to him :
'Even in a bishop I can spy desert ;
Secker is decent ; Rundle has a heart :
Manners with candour are to Benson given,
To Berkeley—every virtue under heaven.'

that few can understand to-day but which will be re-discovered in the future as more pioneer work, too far in advance of its time to be comprehended. As an example I will quote Berkeley's statements :

That which is visible cannot be made up of invisible things,
and
Morality may be demonstrated as mixt mathematics.

I wish Berkeley had written poems on these subjects that I could have included here ; but as far as I can discover he only wrote one poem.

But there were other giants in the eighteenth century. I draw attention to Swift's *Cadenus and Vanessa*, the only long poem I have included in this anthology, which is a perfect example of Swift's sustained power of thought and must be read slowly from start to finish to be properly enjoyed and appreciated. James Thomson is a magnificent poet unduly neglected, and I have tried to represent him briefly but fully ; he is a poet, however, who gets a cumulative effect, and I am not sure how far I have done him justice. William Blake is the only poet represented here who lived on into the nineteenth century, but all his lyrical poetry was written and published before 1800, and every poem in this anthology was written and published between the years 1700 and 1800. These limits exclude Dryden, who died in 1700, and I have let them exclude Coleridge and Wordsworth, for although " Lyrical Ballads " was published in 1798 they belong undisputably to the nineteenth century.

Every good anthology must bear the character of

its editor, which he cannot well know ; but I would claim for this anthology that it contains no padding. I have tried to make it both varied and exclusive and I have not included a single poem I did not admire. A great mass of eighteenth century verse is swamped with conventional description of nature. The reader will, I hope, find none of that here. Let him not think that Thomson's verse is of this kind ! Thomson certainly uses a convention, but with what fire, vigour and felicity ! His descriptions are based on direct experiences of nature, not on literature, and he informs them with his own temper.

Something may be said about technique. The poets of the eighteenth century, with rare exceptions, confined themselves to a few regular forms and these they used strictly. What they lacked in elasticity and variety of syllabic rhythm was, to some extent, compensated for at the hands of the greatest masters by a concentration on vowel and consonantal music. This may be seen to perfection in some of the most celebrated lines of Pope, whose best-known poem *The Rape of the Lock* I have omitted here as being too familiar and too long.

W. J. T.

Contents

ix

CONTENTS

CONTENTS

xi

CONTENTS

CONTENTS

CONTENTS

CONTENTS

CONTENTS

DANIEL DEFOE

1661–1731

Our English Race

THE *Romans* first with *Julius Cæsar* came,
Including all the Nations of that Name,
Gauls, *Greeks*, and *Lombards* ; and by Computation,
Auxiliaries or Slaves of ev'ry Nation.
With *Hengist*, *Saxons* ; *Danes* with *Sueno* came,
In search of Plunder, not in search of Fame.
Scots, *Picts*, and *Irish* from th' *Hibernian* Shore :
And Conqu'ring *William* brought the *Normans* o'er.

All these their Barb'rous Offspring left behind,
The Dregs of Armies, they of all Mankind ;
Blended with *Britains* who before were here,
Of whom the *Welsh* ha' blest the Character.

From this Amphibious Ill-born Mob began
That vain ill-natur'd thing, an Englishman.
The Customs, Sirnames, Languages, and Manners,
Of all these Nations are their own Explainers :
Whose Relicks are so lasting and so strong,
They ha' left a *Shiboleth* upon our Tongue ;
By which with easy search you may distinguish
Your *Roman-Saxon-Danish-Norman* English.

The great Invading *Norman* let us know
What Conquerors in After-Times might do.
To ev'ry * *Musqueteer* he brought to *Town*,
He gave the Lands which never were his own.
When first the *English* Crown he did obtain,
He did not send his *Dutchmen* home again.
No Reassumptions in his Reign were known,
Davenant might there ha' let his Book alone.

* *Or* Archer.

No Parliament his Army cou'd disband ;
He rais'd no Money, for he paid in Land.
He gave his Legions their Eternal Station,
And made them all Freeholders of the Nation.
He canton'd out the Country to his Men,
And ev'ry Soldier was a Denizen.
The Rascals thus enrich'd, he call'd them *Lords,*
To please their Upstart Pride with new-made Words ;
And *Doomsday Book* his Tyranny Records.

And here begins the Ancient Pedigree
That so exalts our Poor Nobility :
'Tis that from some *French* Trooper they derive,
Who with the *Norman* Bastard did arrive :
The Trophies of the Families appear ;
Some show the Sword, the Bow, and some the Spear,
Which their Great Ancestor, *forsooth*, did wear.
These in the Heralds Register remain,
Their Noble mean Extraction to explain.
Yet who the Hero was, no Man can tell,
Whether a Drummer or a Colonel :
The silent Record blushes to reveal
Their Undescended Dark Original.

But grant the best, How came the Change to pass ;
A *True-Born Englishman of Norman* Race ?
A *Turkish* Horse can show more History,
To prove his Well-descended Family.
Conquest, as by the Moderns 'tis exprest,
May give a Title to the Lands possest :
But that the Longest Sword shou'd be so Civil,
To make a *Frenchman English*, that's the Devil.

These are the Heroes who despise the *Dutch,*
And rail at new-come Foreigners so much ;

Forgetting that themselves are all deriv'd
From the most Scoundrel Race that ever liv'd,
A horrid Crowd of Rambling Thieves and Drones,
Who ransack'd Kingdoms, and dispeopled Towns :
The *Pict* and Painted *Britain*, Treach'rous *Scot*,
By Hunger, Theft, and Rapine, hither brought ;
Norwegian Pirates, Buccaneering *Danes*,
Whose Red-hair'd Offspring ev'ry where remains ;
Who join'd with *Norman-French* compound the Breed
From whence your *True-Born Englishmen* proceed.

THE TRUE-BORN ENGLISHMAN.

ANNE, COUNTESS OF WINCHELSEA
1661–1720

A Nocturnal Reverie

In such an *Night*, when every louder Wind
Is to its distant Cavern safe confin'd ;
And only gentle *Zephyr* fans his Wings,
And lonely *Philomel*, still waking, sings ;
Or from some Tree, fam'd for the *Owl's* delight,
She, hollowing clear, directs the Wand'rer right :
In such a *Night*, when passing clouds give place,
Or thinly vail the Heav'ns mysterious Face ;
When in some River, overhung with Green,
The waving Moon and trembling Leaves are seen ;
When freshen'd Grass now bears it self upright,
And makes cool Banks to pleasing Rest invite,
Whence springs the *Woodbind*, and the *Bramble-Rose*,
And where the sleepy *Cowslip* shelter'd grows ;

3

Whilst now a paler Hue the *Foxglove* takes,
Yet chequers still with Red the dusky brakes :
When scatter'd *Glow-worms*, but in Twilight fine,
Shew trivial Beauties, watch their Hour to shine ;
Whilst *Salisb'ry* stands the Test of every Light,
In perfect Charms, and perfect Virtue bright :
When Odours, which declin'd repelling Day,
Thro' temp'rate Air uninterrupted stray ;
When darken'd Groves their softest Shadows wear,
And falling Waters we distinctly hear ;
When thro' the Gloom more venerable shows
Some ancient Fabrick, awful in Repose,
While Sunburnt Hills their swarthy Looks conceal,
And swelling Haycocks thicken up the Vale :
When the loos'd *Horse* now, as his Pasture leads,
Comes slowly grazing thro' th' adjoining Meads,
Whose stealing Pace, and lengthen'd Shade we fear,
Till torn up Forage in his Teeth we hear :
When nibbling *Sheep* at large pursue their Food,
And unmolested Kine rechew the Cud ;
When *Curlews* cry beneath the Village-walls,
And to her straggling Brood the *Partridge* calls ;
Their shortliv'd Jubilee the Creatures keep,
Which but endures, whilst Tyrant-*Man* do's sleep ;
When a sedate Content the Spirit feels,
And no fierce Light disturbs, whilst it reveals ;
But silent Musings urge the Mind to seek
Something, too high for Syllables to speak ;
Till the free Soul to a compos'dness charm'd,
Finding the Elements of Rage disarm'd,
O'er all below a solemn Quiet grown,
Joys in th' inferior World, and thinks it like her Own :

4

WILLIAM WALSH

In such a *Night* let Me abroad remain,
Till Morning breaks, and All's confus'd again ;
Our Cares, our Toils, our Clamours are renew'd,
Or Pleasures, seldom reach'd, again pursu'd.

WILLIAM WALSH

1663–1708

The Reflecting Lover

Distracted with Care,
For *Phillis* the Fair ;
Since nothing cou'd move her,
Poor *Damon*, her Lover,
Resolves in Despair
No longer to languish,
Nor bear so much Anguish ;
But, mad with his Love,
To a Precipice goes ;
Where, a Leap from above
Wou'd soon finish his Woes.

When in Rage he came there,
Beholding how steep
The Sides did appear,
And the Bottom how deep ;
His Torments projecting,
And sadly reflecting,
That a Lover forsaken
A new Love may get ;
But a Neck, when once broken,

5

Can never be set :
And, that he cou'd die
Whenever he wou'd ;
But, that he cou'd live
But as long as he cou'd :
How grievous soever
The Torment might grow,
He scorn'd to endeavour
To finish it so.
But Bold, Unconcern'd
At Thoughts of the Pain,
He calmly return'd
To his Cottage again.

POETICAL MISCELLANIES, V.

MATTHEW PRIOR

1664–1721

An Epitaph

INTERR'D beneath this Marble Stone,
Lie Saunt'ring JACK, and Idle JOAN.
While rolling Threescore Years and One
Did round this Globe their Courses run ;
If Human Things went Ill or Well ;
If changing Empires rose or fell ;
The Morning past, the Evening came,
And found this Couple still the same.
They Walk'd and Eat, good Folks : What then ?
Why then They Walk'd and Eat again :
They soundly slept the Night away :

6

They did just Nothing all the Day :
And having bury'd Children Four,
Wou'd not take Pains to try for more.
Nor Sister either had, nor Brother :
They seem'd just Tally'd for each other.

Their Moral and Oeconomy
Most perfectly They made agree :
Each Virtue kept it's proper Bound,
Nor Trespass'd on the other's Ground.
Nor Fame, nor Censure They regarded :
They neither Punish'd, nor Rewarded.
He car'd not what the Footmen did :
Her Maids She neither prais'd, nor chid :
So ev'ry Servant took his Course ;
And bad at First, They all grew worse.
Slothful Disorder fill'd His Stable ;
And sluttish Plenty deck'd Her Table.
Their Beer was strong ; Their Wine was *Port* ;
Their Meal was large ; Their Grace was short.
They gave the Poor the Remnant-meat,
Just when it grew not fit to eat.

They paid the Church and Parish-Rate ;
And took, but read not the Receit :
For which They claim'd their *Sunday's* Due,
Of slumb'ring in an upper Pew.

No Man's Defects sought They to know ;
So never made Themselves a Foe.
No Man's good Deeds did They commend ;
So never rais'd Themselves a Friend.
Nor cherish'd They Relations poor :
That might decrease Their present Store :
Nor Barn nor House did they repair :

That might oblige Their future Heir.
  They neither Added, nor Confounded :
They neither Wanted, nor Abounded.
Each *Christmas* They Accompts did clear ;
And wound their Bottom round the Year.
Nor Tear, nor Smile did They imploy
At News of Public Grief, or Joy.
When Bells were Rung, and Bonfires made ;
If ask'd, They ne'er deny'd their Aid :
Their Jugg was to the Ringers carry'd ;
Who ever either Dy'd, or Marry'd.
Their Billet at the Fire was found ;
Who ever was Depos'd, or Crown'd.
  Nor Good, nor Bad, nor Fools, nor Wise ;
They wou'd not learn, nor cou'd advise :
Without Love, Hatred, Joy, or Fear,
They led——a kind of——as it were :
Nor Wish'd, nor Car'd, nor Laugh'd, nor Cry'd :
And so They liv'd ; and so They dy'd.

POEMS ON SEVERAL OCCASIONS.

JONATHAN SWIFT

1667–1745

Stella's Birth-day

THIS Day, whate'er the Fates decree,
Shall still be kept with Joy by me :
This Day then, let us not be told,
That you are sick, and I grown old,

Bottom] skein.

8

Nor think on our approaching Ills,
And talk of Spectacles and Pills ;
To morrow will be Time enough
To hear such mortifying Stuff.
Yet, since from Reason may be brought
A better and more pleasing Thought,
Which can, in spite of all Decays,
Support a few remaining Days :
From not the gravest of Divines,
Accept for once some serous Lines.

Although we now can form no more
Long Schemes of Life, as heretofore ;
Yet, you, while Time is running fast,
Can look with Joy on what is past.

Were future Happiness and Pain
A mere Contrivance of the Brain,
As Atheists argue, to entice,
And fit their Proselytes for Vice ;
(The only Comfort they propose,
To have Companions in their Woes)
Grant this the Case, yet sure 'tis hard,
That Virtue, stil'd its own Reward,
And by all Sages understood
To be the chief of human Good,
Should acting, die, not leave behind
Some lasting Pleasure in the Mind,
Which by remembrance will assuage,
Grief, Sickness, Poverty, and Age ;
And strongly shoot a radiant Dart,
To shine through Life's declining Part.

Say, *Stella*, feel you no content,
Reflecting on a Life well spent ?

Your skilful Hand employ'd to save
Despairing Wretches from the Grave ;
And then supporting, with your Store,
Those whom you dragg'd from Death before :
(So Providence on Mortals waits,
Preserving what it first creates)
Your gen'rous Boldness to defend
An innocent and absent Friend :
That Courage which can make you just
To Merit humbled in the Dust :
The Detestation you express
For Vice in all its glitt'ring Dress :
That Patience under tort'ring Pain,
Where stubborn Stoicks would complain.

Must these like empty Shadows pass,
Or Forms reflected from a Glass ?
Or mere Chimaera's in the Mind,
That fly and leave no Marks behind ?
Does not the Body thrive and grow
By Food of twenty Years ago ?
And, had it not been still supply'd,
It must a thousand Times have dy'd.
Then, who with Reason can maintain,
That no Effects of Food remain ?
And, is not Virtue in Mankind
The Nutriment that feeds the Mind ?
Upheld by each good Action past,
And still continued by the last :
Then, who with Reason can pretend,
That all Effects of Virtue end ?

Believe me *Stella*, when you show
That true Contempt for Things below,

Nor prize your Life for other Ends
Than merely to oblige your Friends ;
Your former Actions claim their Part,
And join to fortify your Heart.
For Virtue in her daily Race,
Like *Janus*, bears a double Face ;
Looks back with Joy where she has gone,
And therefore goes with Courage on.
She at your sickly Couch will wait,
And guide you to a better State.

O then, whatever Heav'n intends,
Take Pity on your pitying Friends :
Nor let your Ills affect your Mind,
To fancy they can be unkind.
Me, surely me, you ought to spare,
Who gladly would your Suff'rings share ;
Or give my Scrap of Life to you,
And think it far beneath your Due ;
You, to whose Care so oft I owe,
That I'm alive to tell you so.

On Censure

Ye wise, instruct me to endure
An evil, which admits no cure ;
Or, how this evil can be borne,
Which breeds at once both hate and scorn.
Bare innocence is no support,
When you are tried in Scandal's court.
Stand high in honour, wealth, or wit ;

All others, who inferior sit,
Conceive themselves in conscience bound
To join, and drag you to the ground.
Your altitude offends the eyes
Of those who want the power to rise.
The world, a willing stander-by,
Inclines to aid a specious lie :
Alas ! they would not do you wrong ;
But all appearances are strong.

Yet whence proceeds this weight we lay
On what detracting people say !
For let mankind discharge their tongues
In venom, till they burst their lungs,
Their utmost malice cannot make
Your head, or tooth, or finger ache ;
Nor spoil your shape, distort your face,
Or put one feature out of place ;
Nor will you find your fortune sink
By what they speak or what they think ;
Nor can ten hundred thousand lies
Make you less virtuous, learn'd or wise,

The most effectual way to balk
Their malice, is—to let them talk.

From *On Poetry*

HOBBES clearly proves, that every creature
Lives in a state of war by nature.
The greater for the smaller watch,
But meddle seldom with their match.

A whale of moderate size will draw
A shoal of herrings down his maw ;
A fox with geese his belly crams ;
A wolf destroys a thousand lambs ;
But search among the rhyming race,
The brave are worried by the base.
If on Parnassus' top you sit,
You rarely bite, are always bit :
Each poet of inferior size
On you shall rail and criticize,
And strive to tear you limb from limb ;
While others do as much for him.
  The vermin only teaze and pinch
Their foes superior by an inch.
So naturalists observe, a flea
Has smaller fleas that on him prey ;
And these have smaller still to bite 'em,
And so proceed *ad infinitum*.
Thus every poet, in his kind,
Is bit by him that comes behind :
Who, though too little to be seen,
Can teaze, and gall, and give the spleen ;
Call dunces, fools, and sons of whores,
Lay Grub Street at each other's doors ;
Extol the Greek and Roman masters,
And curse our modern poetasters ;
Complain, as many an ancient bard did,
How genius is no more rewarded ;
How wrong a taste prevails among us ;
How much our ancestors outsung us :
Can personate an awkward scorn
For those who are not poets born ;

And all their brother dunces lash,
Who crowd the press with hourly trash.

Cadenus and Vanessa

THE shepherds and the nymphs were seen
Pleading before the Cyprian queen.
The counsel for the fair began,
Accusing the false creature Man.
The brief with weighty crimes was charged
On which the pleader much enlarged ;
That Cupid now has lost his art,
Or blunts the point of every dart ;
His altar now no longer smokes,
His mother's aid no youth invokes :
This tempts freethinkers to refine,
And bring in doubt their powers divine ;
Now love is dwindled to intrigue,
And marriage grown a money league ;
Which crimes aforesaid (with her leave)
Were (as he humbly did conceive)
Against our sovereign lady's peace,
Against the statute in that case,
Against her dignity and crown :
Then pray'd an answer, and sat down.

The nymphs with scorn beheld their foes ;
When the defendant's counsel rose,
And, what no lawyer ever lack'd,
With impudence own'd all the fact ;

But, what the gentlest heart would vex,
Laid all the fault on t'other sex.
That modern love is no such thing
As what those ancient poets sing :
A fire celestial, chaste, refined,
Conceived and kindled in the mind ;
Which, having found an equal flame,
Unites, and both become the same,
In different breasts together burn,
Together both to ashes turn.
But women now feel no such fire,
And only know the gross desire.
Their passions move in lower spheres,
Where'er caprice or folly steers,
A dog, a parrot, or an ape,
Or some worse brute in human shape,
Engross the fancies of the fair,
The few soft moments they can spare,
From visits to receive and pay,
From scandal, politics, and play ;
From fans, and flounces, and brocades,
From equipage and park parades,
From all the thousand female toys,
From every trifle that employs
The out or inside of their heads,
Between their toilets and their beds.

 In a dull stream, which moving slow,
You hardly see the current flow ;
If a small breeze obstruct the course,
It whirls about, for want of force,
And in its narrow circle gathers
Nothing but chaff, and straws, and feathers.

The current of a female mind
Stops thus, and turns with every wind :
Thus whirling round together draws
Fools, fops, and rakes, for chaff and straws.
Hence we conclude, no women's hearts
Are won by virtue, wit, and parts :
Nor are the men of sense to blame,
For breasts incapable of flame ;
The faults must on the nymphs be placed
Grown so corrupted in their taste.
    The pleader having spoke his best,
Had witness ready to attest,
Who fairly could on oath depose,
When questions on the fact arose,
That every article was true ;
Nor further those deponents knew :
Therefore he humbly would insist,
The bill might be with costs dismiss'd.

The cause appear'd of so much weight,
That Venus, from her judgement seat,
Desired them not to talk so loud,
Else she must interpose a cloud :
For if the heavenly folks should know
These pleadings in the courts below,
That mortals here disdain to love,
She ne'er could show her face above ;
For gods, their betters, are too wise
To value that which men despise.
And then, said she, my son and I
Must stroll in air, 'twixt land and sky ;
Or else, shut out from heaven and earth,

Fly to the sea, my place of birth :
There live with daggled mermaids pent,
And keep on fish perpetual Lent.
  But since the case appear'd so nice,
She thought it best to take advice.

The Muses by the king's permission,
Though foes to love, attend the session,
And on the right hand took their places
In order ; on the left, the Graces :
To whom she might her doubts propose
On all emergencies that rose.
The Muses oft were seen to frown ;
The Graces half ashamed look'd down ;
And 'twas observed, there were but few
Of either sex among the crew,
Whom she or her assessors knew.
The goddess soon began to see,
Things were not ripe for a decree ;
And said, she must consult her books,
The lovers' Fletas, Bractons, Cokes.
First to a dapper clerk she beckon'd
To turn to Ovid, book the second :
She then referr'd them to a place
In Virgil, *vide* Dido's case :
As for Tibullus's reports,
They never passed for law in courts :
For Cowley's briefs, and pleas of Waller,
Still their authority was smaller.
  There was on both sides much to say :
She'd hear the cause another day ;
And so she did ; and then a third ;

She heard it—there she kept her word :
But, with rejoinders or replies,
Long bills, and answers stuff'd with lies,
Demur, imparlance, and essoign,
The parties ne'er could issue join :
For sixteen years the cause was spun,
And then stood where it first begun.

Now, gentle Clio, sing, or say
What Venus meant by this delay ?
The goddess much perplex'd in mind
To see her empire thus declined,
When first this grand debate arose,
Above her wisdom to compose,
Conceived a project in her head
To work her ends ; which, if it sped,
Would show the merits of the cause
Far better than consulting laws.
In a glad hour Lucina's aid
Produced on earth a wondrous maid,
On whom the Queen of Love was bent
To try a new experiment.
She threw her law-books on the shelf,
And thus debated with herself.
Since men allege, they ne'er can find
Those beauties in a female mind,
Which raise a flame that will endure
For ever uncorrupt and pure ;
If 'tis with reason they complain,
This infant shall restore my reign.
I'll search where every virtue dwells,
From courts inclusive down to cells :

What preachers talk, or sages write;
These will I gather and unite,
And represent them to mankind
Collected in that infant's mind.

   This said, she plucks in Heaven's high bowers
A sprig of amaranthine flowers.
In nectar thrice infuses bays,
Three times refined in Titan's rays;
Then calls the Graces to her aid,
And sprinkles thrice the newborn maid:
From whence the tender skin assumes
A sweetness above all perfumes:
From whence a cleanliness remains,
Incapable of outward stains:
From whence that decency of mind,
So lovely in the female kind,
Where not one careless thought intrudes;
Less modest than the speech of prudes;
Where never blush was call'd in aid,
That spurious virtue in a maid,
A virtue but at second-hand;
They blush because they understand.

   The Graces next would act their part,
And show'd but little of their art;
Their work was half already done,
The child with native beauty shone;
The outward form no help required:
Each, breathing on her thrice, inspired
That gentle, soft, engaging air,
Which in old times adorn'd the fair:
And said, "Vanessa be the name
By which thou shalt be known to fame:

Vanessa, by the gods enroll'd :
Her name on earth shall not be told."

But still the work was not complete ;
When Venus thought on a deceit.
Drawn by her doves, away she flies,
And finds out Pallas in the skies.
Dear Pallas, I have been this morn
To see a lovely infant born :
A boy in yonder isle below,
So like my own without his bow,
By beauty could your heart be won,
You'd swear it is Apollo's son ;
But it shall ne'er be said, a child
So hopeful, has by me been spoil'd :
I have enough besides to spare,
And give him wholly to your care.
Wisdom's above suspecting wiles ;
The Queen of Learning gravely smiles,
Down from Olympus comes with joy,
Mistakes Vanessa for a boy ;
Then sows within her tender mind
Seeds long unknown to womankind :
For manly bosoms chiefly fit,
The seeds of knowledge, judgement, wit.
Her soul was suddenly endued
With justice, truth, and fortitude ;
With honour, which no breath can stain,
Which malice must attack in vain ;
With open heart and bounteous hand.
But Pallas here was at a stand ;
She knew, in our degenerate days,

Bare virtue could not live on praise ;
That meat must be with money bought :
She therefore, upon second thought,
Infused, yet as it were by stealth,
Some small regard for state and wealth ;
Of which, as she grew up, there staid
A tincture in the prudent maid :
She managed her estate with care,
Yet liked three footmen to her chair.
But, lest he should neglect his studies
Like a young heir, the thrifty goddess
(For fear young master should be spoil'd)
Would use him like a younger child ;
And, after long computing, found
'Twould come to just five thousand pound.

The Queen of Love was pleased, and proud,
To see Vanessa thus endow'd :
She doubted not but such a dame
Through every breast would dart a flame,
That every rich and lordly swain
With pride would drag about her chain ;
That scholars would forsake their books,
To study bright Vanessa's looks ;
As she advanced, that womankind
Would by her model form their mind,
And all their conduct would be tried
By her, as an unerring guide ;
Offending daughters oft would hear
Vanessa's praise rung in their ear :
Miss Betty, when she does a fault,
Lets fall her knife, or spills the salt,

Will thus be by her mother chid,
" 'Tis what Vanessa never did ! "
Thus by the nymphs and swains adored,
My power shall be again restored,
And happy lovers bless my reign—
So Venus hoped, but hoped in vain.

For when in time the Martial Maid
Found out the trick that Venus play'd,
She shakes her helm, she knits her brows,
And, fired with indignation, vows,
To-morrow, ere the setting sun,
She'd all undo that she had done.

But in the poets we may find
A wholesome law, time out of mind,
Had been confirm'd by Fate's decree,
That gods, of whatsoe'er degree,
Resume not what themselves have given,
Or any brother god in Heaven :
Which keeps the peace among the gods,
Or they must always be at odds :
And Pallas, if she broke the laws,
Must yield her foe the stronger cause ;
A shame to one so much adored
For wisdom at Jove's council-board.
Besides, she fear'd the Queen of Love
Would meet with better friends above.
And though she must with grief reflect,
To see a mortal virgin deck'd
With graces hitherto unknown
To female breasts, except her own :
Yet she would act as best became
A goddess of unspotted fame.

She knew, by augury divine,
Venus would fail in her design :
She studied well the point, and found
Her foe's conclusions were not sound,
From premises erroneous brought,
And therefore the deduction's naught,
And must have contrary effects,
To what her treacherous foe expects.

In proper season Pallas meets
The Queen of Love, whom thus she greets,
(For gods, we are by Homer told,
Can in celestial language scold :)—
Perfidious goddess ! but in vain
You form'd this project in your brain ;
A project for your talents fit,
With much deceit and little wit.
Thou hast, as thou shalt quickly see,
Deceived thyself, instead of me ;
For how can heavenly wisdom prove
An instrument to earthly love ?
Know'st thou not yet, that men commence
Thy votaries for want of sense ?
Nor shall Vanessa be the theme
To manage thy abortive scheme :
She'll prove the greatest of thy foes ;
And yet I scorn to interpose,
But, using neither skill nor force,
Leave all things to their natural course.
  The goddess thus pronounced her doom :
When, lo ! Vanessa in her bloom
Advanced, like Atalanta's star,

But rarely seen, and seen from far :
In a new world with caution stept,
Watch'd all the company she kept,
Well knowing, from the books she read,
What dangerous paths young virgins tread :
Would seldom at the Park appear,
Nor saw the play-house twice a year ;
Yet, not incurious, was inclined
To know the converse of mankind.

First issued from perfumer's shops,
A crowd of fashionable fops :
They ask'd her how she liked the play ;
Then told the tattle of the day ;
A duel fought last night at two,
About a lady—you know who ;
Mention'd a new Italian, come
Either from Muscovy or Rome ;
Gave hints of who and who's together ;
Then fell to talking of the weather ;
Last night was so extremely fine,
The ladies walk'd till after nine :
Then, in soft voice and speech absurd,
With nonsense every second word,
With fustian from exploded plays,
They celebrate her beauty's praise ;
Run o'er their cant of stupid lies,
And tell the murders of her eyes.
  With silent scorn Vanessa sat,
Scarce listening to their idle chat ;
Farther than sometimes by a frown,
When they grew pert, to pull them down.

At last she spitefully was bent
To try their wisdom's full extent ;
And said, she valued nothing less
Than titles, figure, shape, and dress ;
That merit should be chiefly placed
In judgement, knowledge, wit, and taste ;
And these, she offer'd to dispute,
Alone distinguish'd man from brute :
That present times have no pretence
To virtue, in the noble sense
By Greeks and Romans understood,
To perish for our country's good.
She named the ancient heroes round,
Explain'd for what they were renown'd ;
Then spoke with censure or applause
Of foreign customs, rites, and laws ;
Through nature and through art she ranged
And gracefully her subject changed ;
In vain ! her hearers had no share
In all she spoke, except to stare.
Their judgement was, upon the whole,
—That lady is the dullest soul !—
Then tapt their forehead in a jeer,
As one would say—She wants it here !
She may be handsome, young, and rich,
But none will burn her for a witch !

A party next of glittering dames,
From round the purlieus of St. James,
Came early, out of pure good will,
To see the girl in dishabille.
Their clamour, 'lighting from their chairs

Grew louder all the way up stairs ;
At entrance loudest, where they found
The room with volumes litter'd round.
Vanessa held Montaigne, and read,
While Mrs. Susan comb'd her head.
They call'd for tea and chocolate,
And fell into their usual chat,
Discoursing with important face,
On ribbons, fans, and gloves, and lace ;
Show'd patterns just from India brought,
And gravely ask'd her what she thought,
Whether the red or green were best,
And what they cost ? Vanessa guess'd
As came into her fancy first ;
Named half the rates, and liked the worst.
To scandal next—What awkward thing
Was that last Sunday in the ring ?
I'm sorry Mopsa breaks so fast :
I said her face would never last.
Corinna, with that youthful air,
Is thirty, and a bit to spare :
Her fondness for a certain earl
Began when I was but a girl !
Phillis, who but a month ago
Was married to the Tunbridge beau,
I saw coquetting t'other night
In public with that odious knight !
They rallied next Vanessa's dress :
That gown was made for old Queen Bess.
Dear madam, let me see your head :
Don't you intend to put on red ?
A petticoat without a hoop !

Sure, you are not ashamed to stoop !
With handsome garters at your knees,
No matter what a fellow sees.
  Fill'd with disdain, with rage inflamed
Both of herself and sex ashamed,
The nymph stood silent out of spite,
Nor would vouchsafe to set them right.
Away the fair detractors went,
And gave by turns their censures vent.
She's not so handsome in my eyes :
For wit, I wonder where it lies !
She's fair and clean, and that's the most :
But why proclaim her for a toast ?
A baby face ; no life, no airs,
But what she learn'd at country fairs ;
Scarce knows what difference is between
Rich Flanders lace and Colberteen.[1]
I'll undertake, my little Nancy
In flounces has a better fancy ;
With all her wit, I would not ask
Her judgement how to buy a mask.
We begg'd her but to patch her face,
She never hit one proper place ;
Which every girl at five years old
Can do as soon as she is told.
I own, that out-of-fashion stuff
Becomes the creature well enough.
The girl might pass, if we could get her
To know the world a little better.

[1] A lace so called after the celebrated French Minister, Colbert.
Planché's *British Costume.*

(To know the world ! a modern phrase
For visits, ombre, balls, and plays.)

Thus, to the world's perpetual shame,
The Queen of Beauty lost her aim ;
Too late with grief she understood
Pallas had done more harm than good ;
For great examples are but vain,
Where ignorance begets disdain.
Both sexes, arm'd with guilt and spite,
Against Vanessa's power unite :
To copy her few nymphs aspired ;
Her virtues fewer swains admired.
So stars, beyond a certain height,
Give mortals neither heat nor light.
Yet some of either sex, endow'd
With gifts superior to the crowd,
With virtue, knowledge, taste, and wit
She condescended to admit :
With pleasing arts she could reduce
Men's talents to their proper use ;
And with address each genius held
To that wherein it most excell'd ;
Thus, making others' widsom known,
Could please them, and improve her own.
A modest youth said something new ;
She placed it in the strongest view.
All humble worth she strove to raise,
Would not be praised, yet loved to praise.
The learned met with free approach,
Although they came not in a coach :
Some clergy too she would allow,

Nor quarrell'd at their awkward bow ;
But this was for Cadenus' sake,
A gownman of a different make ;
Whom Pallas once, Vanessa's tutor,
Had fix'd on for her coadjutor.
  But Cupid, full of mischief, longs
To vindicate his mother's wrongs.
On Pallas all attempts are vain :
One way he knows to give her pain ;
Vows on Vanessa's heart to take
Due vengeance, for her patron's sake ;
Those early seeds by Venus sown,
In spite of Pallas now were grown ;
And Cupid hoped they would improve
By time, and ripen into love.
The boy made use of all his craft,
In vain discharging many a shaft,
Pointed at colonels, lords, and beaux :
Cadenus warded off the blows ;
For, placing still some book betwixt,
The darts were in the cover fix'd,
Or, often blunted and recoil'd,
On Plutarch's Moral struck, were spoil'd.

  The Queen of Wisdom could foresee,
But not prevent, the Fate's decree :
And human caution tries in vain
To break the adamantine chain.
Vanessa, though by Pallas taught,
By Love invulnerable thought,
Searching in books for wisdom's aid,
Was, in the very search betray'd.

Cupid, though all his darts were lost,
Yet still resolved to spare no cost :
He could not answer to his fame
The triumphs of that stubborn dame,
A nymph so hard to be subdued,
Who neither was coquette nor prude.
I find, said he, she wants a doctor,
Both to adore her, and instruct her :
I'll give her what she most admires
Among those venerable sires.
Cadenus is a subject fit,
Grown old in politics and wit,
Caress'd by ministers of state,
Of half mankind the dread and hate.
Whate'er vexations love attend,
She needs no rivals apprehend.
Her sex, with universal voice,
Must laugh at her capricious choice.

Cadenus many things had writ :
Vanessa much esteem'd his wit,
And call'd for his poetic works :
Meantime the boy in secret lurks ;
And, while the book was in her hand,
The urchin from his private stand
Took aim, and shot with all his strength
A dart of such prodigious length,
It pierced the feeble volume through,
And deep transfix'd her bosom too.
Some lines, more moving than the rest,
Stuck to the point that pierced her breast,
And, borne directly to the heart,
With pains unknown increased her smart.

Vanessa, not in years a score,
Dreams of a gown of forty-four ;
Imaginary charms can find
In eyes with reading almost blind :
Cadenus now no more appears
Declined in health, advanced in years.
She fancies music in his tongue ;
Nor farther looks, but thinks him young.
What mariner is not afraid
To venture in a ship decay'd ?
What planter will attempt to yoke
A sapling with a falling oak ?
As years increase, she brighter shines ;
Cadenus with each day declines :
And he must fall a prey to time,
While she continues in her prime.
Cadenus, common forms apart,
In every scene had kept his heart ;
Had sigh'd and languish'd, vow'd and writ,
For pastime, or to show his wit,
But books, and time, and state affairs,
Had spoil'd his fashionable airs :
He now could praise, esteem, approve,
But understood not what was love.
His conduct might have made him styled
A father, and the nymph his child.
That innocent delight he took
To see the virgin mind her book,
Was but the master's secret joy
In school to hear the finest boy.
Her knowledge with her fancy grew ;
She hourly press'd for something new ;

Ideas came into her mind
So fast, his lessons lagg'd behind ;
She reason'd, without plodding long,
Nor ever gave her judgement wrong.
But now a sudden change was wrought ;
She minds no longer what he taught.
Cadenus was amazed to find
Such marks of a distracted mind :
For, though she seem'd to listen more
To all he spoke, than e'er before,
He found her thoughts would absent range,
Yet guess'd not whence could spring the change.
And first he modestly conjectures
His pupil might be tired with lectures ;
Which help'd to mortify his pride,
Yet gave him not the heart to chide :
But, in a mild dejected strain,
At last he ventured to complain :
Said, she should be no longer teazed,
Might have her freedom when she pleased ;
Was now convinced he acted wrong
To hide her from the world so long,
And in dull studies to engage
One of her tender sex and age ;
That every nymph with envy own'd,
How she might shine in the *grand monde* :
And every shepherd was undone
To see her cloister'd like a nun.
This was a visionary scheme :
He waked, and found it but a dream ;
A project far above his skill :
For nature must be nature still.

If he were bolder than became
A scholar to a courtly dame,
She might excuse a man of letters ;
Thus tutors often treat their betters ;
And, since his talk offensive grew,
He came to take his last adieu.

Vanessa, fill'd with just disdain,
Would still her dignity maintain,
Instructed from her early years
To scorn the art of female tears.
Had he employ'd his time so long
To teach her what was right and wrong ;
Yet could such notions entertain
That all his lectures were in vain ?
She own'd the wandering of her thoughts ;
But he must answer for her faults.
She well remember'd to her cost,
That all his lessons were not lost.
Two maxims she could still produce,
And sad experience taught their use ;
That virtue, pleased by being shown,
Knows nothing which it dares not own ;
Can make us without fear disclose
Our inmost secrets to our foes ;
That common forms were not design'd
Directors to a noble mind.
Now, said the nymph, to let you see
My actions with your rules agree ;
That I can vulgar forms despise,
And have no secrets to disguise ;
I knew, by what you said and writ,

How dangerous things were men of wit ;
You caution'd me against their charms,
But never gave me equal arms ;
Your lessons found the weakest part,
Aim'd at the head, but reach'd the heart.
  Cadenus felt within him rise
Shame, disappointment, guilt, surprise.
He knew not how to reconcile
Such language with her usual style :
And yet her words were so exprest,
He could not hope she spoke in jest.
His thoughts had wholly been confined
To form and cultivate her mind.
He hardly knew, till he was told,
Whether the nymph were young or old ;
Had met her in a public place,
Without distinguishing her face ;
Much less could his declining age
Vanessa's earliest thoughts engage ;
And, if her youth indifference met,
His person must contempt beget ;
Or grant her passion be sincere,
How shall his innocence be clear ?
[1] Appearances were all so strong,
The world must think him in the wrong ;
Would say, he made a treacherous use
Of wit, to flatter and seduce ;
The town would swear, he had betray'd
By magic spells the harmless maid :
And every beau would have his joke,
That scholars were like other folk ;

[1] See the verses " On Censure."

And, when Platonic flights were over,
The tutor turn'd a mortal lover !
So tender of the young and fair !
It show'd a true paternal care—
Five thousand guineas in her purse !
The doctor might have fancied worse.

Hardly at length he silence broke,
And falter'd every word he spoke ;
Interpreting her complaisance,
Just as a man *sans* consequence.
She rallied well, he always knew :
Her manner now was something new ;
And what she spoke was in an air
As serious as a tragic player.
But those who aim at ridicule
Should fix upon some certain rule,
Which faintly hints they are in jest,
Else he must enter his protest :
For let a man be ne'er so wise,
He may be caught with sober lies ;
A science which he never taught,
And, to be free, was dearly bought ;
For, take it in its proper light,
'Tis just what coxcombs call a bite.
But, not to dwell on things minute,
Vanessa finish'd the dispute ;
Brought weighty arguments to prove
That reason was her guide in love.
She thought she had himself described,
His doctrines when she first imbibed ;
What he had planted, now was grown ;

His virtues she might call her own ;
As he approves, as he dislikes,
Love or contempt her fancy strikes.
Self-love, in nature rooted fast,
Attends us first, and leaves us last ;
Why she likes him, admire not at her ;
She loves herself, and that's the matter.
How was her tutor wont to praise
The geniuses of ancient days !
(Those authors he so oft had named,
For learning, wit, and wisdom, famed ;)
Was struck with love, esteem, and awe,
For persons whom he never saw.
Suppose Cadenus flourish'd then,
He must adore such godlike men.
If one short volume could comprise
All that was witty, learn'd, and wise,
How would it be esteem'd and read,
Although the writer long were dead !
If such an author were alive,
How all would for his friendship strive,
And come in crowds to see his face !
And this she takes to be her case.
Cadenus answers every end,
The book, the author, and the friend ;
The utmost her desires will reach,
Is but to learn what he can teach :
His converse is a system fit
Alone to fill up all her wit ;
While every passion of her mind
In him is centred and confined.

Love can with speech inspire a mute,
And taught Vanessa to dispute.
This topic, never touch'd before,
Display'd her eloquence the more :
Her knowledge, with such pains acquired,
By this new passion grew inspired ;
Through this she made all objects pass,
Which gave a tincture o'er the mass ;
As rivers, though they bend and twine,
Still to the sea their course incline :
Or, as philosophers, who find
Some favourite system to their mind ;
In every point to make it fit,
Will force all nature to submit.

Cadenus, who could ne'er suspect
His lessons would have such effect,
Or be so artfully applied,
Insensibly came on her side.
It was an unforeseen event ;
Things took a turn he never meant.
Whoe'er excels in what we prize,
Appears a hero in our eyes ;
Each girl, when pleased with what is taught,
Will have the teacher in her thought.
When miss delights in her spinet,
A fiddler may a fortune get ;
A blockhead, with melodious voice,
In boarding-schools may have his choice ;
And oft the dancing-master's art
Climbs from the toe to touch the heart.
In learning let a nymph delight,
The pedant gets a mistress by't.

Cadenus, to his grief and shame,
Could scarce oppose Vanessa's flame ;
And, though her arguments were strong,
At least could hardly wish them wrong.
Howe'er it came, he could not tell,
But sure she never talk'd so well.
His pride began to interpose ;
Preferr'd before a crowd of beaux !
So bright a nymph to come unsought !
Such wonder by his merit wrought !
'Tis merit must with her prevail !
He never knew her judgement fail !
She noted all she ever read !
And had a most discerning head !

'Tis an old maxim in the schools,
That flattery's the food of fools ;
Yet now and then your men of wit
Will condescend to take a bit.
So when Cadenus could not hide,
He chose to justify his pride ;
Construing the passion she had shown,
Much to her praise, more to his own.
Nature in him had merit placed,
In her a most judicious taste.
Love, hitherto a transient guest,
Ne'er held possession of his breast ;
So long attending at the gate,
Disdain'd to enter in so late.
Love why do we one passion call,
When 'tis a compound of them all ?
Where hot and cold, where sharp and sweet,

In all their equipages meet ;
Where pleasures mix'd with pains appear,
Sorrow with joy, and hope with fear ;
Wherein his dignity and age
Forbid Cadenus to engage.
But friendship, in its greatest height,
A constant, rational delight,
On virtue's basis fix'd to last,
When love allurements long are past,
Which gently warms, but cannot burn,
He gladly offers in return ;
His want of passion will redeem
With gratitude, respect, esteem :
With what devotion we bestow,
When goddesses appear below.
  While thus Cadenus entertains
Vanessa in exalted strains,
The nymph in sober words entreats
A truce with all sublime conceits ;
For why such raptures, flights, and fancies,
To her who durst not read romances ?
In lofty style to make replies,
Which he had taught her to despise ?
But when her tutor will affect
Devotion, duty, and respect,
He fairly abdicates the throne :
The government is now her own ;
He has a forfeiture incurr'd ;
She vows to take him at his word,
And hopes he will not think it strange,
If both should now their stations change,
The nymph will have her turn to be

The tutor ; and the pupil, he ;
Though she already can discern
Her scholar is not apt to learn ;
Or wants capacity to reach
The science she designs to teach ;
Wherein his genius was below
The skill of every common beau,
Who, though he cannot spell, is wise
Enough to read a lady's eyes,
And will each accidental glance
Interpret for a kind advance.

But what success Vanessa met,
Is to the world a secret yet.
Whether the nymph, to please her swain,
Talks in a high romantic strain ;
Or whether he at last descends
To act with less seraphic ends ;
Or to compound the business, whether
They temper love and books together ;
Must never to mankind be told,
Nor shall the conscious Muse unfold.
Meantime the mournful Queen of Love
Led but a weary life above.
She ventures now to leave the skies,
Grown by Vanessa's conduct wise :
For though by one perverse event
Pallas had cross'd her first intent ;
Though her design was not obtain'd :
Yet had she much experience gain'd,
And, by the project vainly tried,
Could better now the cause decide.

She gave due notice, that both parties,
Coram Regina, prox' die Martis,
Should at their peril, without fail,
Come and appear, and save their bail.
All met ; and silence thrice proclaim'd,
One lawyer to each side was named.
The judge discover'd in her face
Resentments for her late disgrace ;
And full of anger, shame, and grief,
Directed them to mind their brief ;
Nor spend their time to show their reading :
She'd have a summary proceeding.
She gather'd under every head
The sum of what each lawyer said,
Gave her own reasons last, and then
Decreed the cause against the men.
    But in weighty case like this,
To show she did not judge amiss,
Which evil tongues might else report,
She made a speech in open court ;
Wherein she grievously complains,
" How she was cheated by the swains ;
On whose petition (humbly showing,
That women were not worth the wooing,
And that, unless the sex would mend,
The race of lovers soon must end)—
She was at Lord knows what expense
To form a nymph of wit and sense,
A model for her sex design'd,
Who never could one lover find.
She saw her favour was misplaced ;
The fellows had a wretched taste ;

She needs must tell them to their face,
They were a stupid, senseless race ;
And, were she to begin again,
She'd study to reform the men ;
Or add some grains of folly more
To women, than they had before,
To put them on an equal foot ;
And this, or nothing else, would do't.
This might their mutual fancy strike ;
Since every being loves its like.
 " But now, repenting what was done,
She left all business to her son ;
She put the world in his possession,
And let him use it at discretion."
 The crier was order'd to dismiss
The court, who made his last " O yes ! "
The goddess would no longer wait ;
But, rising from her chair of state,
Left all below at six and seven,
Harness'd her doves, and flew to Heaven.

From *To Dr. Delany*

Dame Nature, as the learned show,
Provides each animal its foe :
Hounds hunt the hare, the wily fox
Devours your geese, the wolf your flocks.
Thus envy pleads a natural claim
To persecute the Muse's fame ;
On poets in all times abusive,

From Homer down to Pope inclusive.
  Yet what avails it to complain?
You try to take revenge in vain.
A rat your utmost rage defies,
That safe behind the wainscot lies.
Say, did you ever know by sight
In cheese an individual mite!
Show me the same numeric flea,
That bit your neck but yesterday.
    .   .   .   .   .

On me when dunces are satiric,
I take it for a panegyric.
Hated by fools, and fools to hate,
Be that my motto, and my fate.

Verses on the Death of Dr. Swift

Written by Himself : November, 1731

THE time is not remote, when I
Must by the course of nature die;
When, I foresee, my special friends
Will try to find their private ends:
And though 'tis hardly understood
Which way my death can do them good,
Yet thus, methinks, I hear them speak:
' See how the Dean begins to break!
' Poor gentleman, he droops apace!
' You plainly find it in his face.
' That old vertigo in his head
' Will never leave him, till he's dead.

' Besides, his memory decays :
' He recollects not what he says ;
' He cannot call his friends to mind ;
' Forgets the place where last he din'd ;
' Plies you with stories o'er and o'er ;
' He told them fifty times before.
' How does he fancy we can sit
' To hear his out-of-fashion wit ?
' But he takes up with younger folks,
' Who for his wine will bear his jokes.
' Faith ! he must make his stories shorter,
' Or change his comrades once a quarter :
' In half the time he talks them round,
' There must another set be found.
 ' For poetry, he's past his prime :
' He takes an hour to find a rhyme ;
' His fire is out, his wit decay'd,
' His fancy sunk, his Muse a jade.
' I'd have him throw away his pen ;—
' But there's no talking to some men ! '
 And then their tenderness appears
By adding largely to my years :
' He's older than he would be reckon'd,
' And well remembers *Charles* the Second.
' He hardly drinks a pint of wine ;
' And that, I doubt, is no good sign.
' His stomach too begins to fail :
' Last year we thought him strong and hale :
' But now he's quite another thing :
'I wish he may hold out till spring ! '
They hug themselves, and reason thus :
' It is not yet so bad with us ! '

In such a case, they talk in tropes,
And by their fears express their hopes.
Some great misfortune to portend,
No enemy can match a friend.
With all the kindness they profess,
The merit of a luckly guess
(When daily *Howd'y's* come of course,
And servants answer ' Worse and worse ! ')
Would please them better, than to tell,
That, ' God be prais'd, the Dean is well.'
Then he, who prophesied the best,
Approves his foresight to the rest :
' You know I always fear'd the worst,
' And often told you so at first.'
He'd rather choose that I should die,
Than his predictions prove a lie.
Not one foretells I shall recover ;
But all agree to give me over.

  .   .   .   .   .

 Behold the fatal day arrive !
' How is the Dean ? '—' He's just alive.'
Now the departing prayer is read ;
' He hardly breathes '—' The Dean is dead.'
 Before the passing-bell begun,
The news through half the town is run.
' O ! may we all for death prepare !
' What has he left ? and who's his heir ?
' I know no more than what the news is ;
' 'Tis all bequeath'd to publick uses.
' To publick uses ! there's a whim !
' What had the publick done for him ?
' Mere envy, avarice, and pride :

' He gave it all—but first he died.
' And had the Dean, in all the nation,
' No worthy friend, no poor relation ?
' So ready to do strangers good,
' Forgetting his own flesh and blood ! '

Now Grubstreet wits are all employ'd ;
With elegies the town is cloy'd :
Some paragraph in every paper,
To *curse* the *Dean*, or *bless* the *Drapier*.

The doctors, tender of their fame,
Wisely on me lay all the blame.
' We must confess, his case was nice ;
' But he would never take advice.
' Had he been rul'd, for aught appears,
' He might have liv'd these twenty years :
' For, when we open'd him, we found,
' That all his vital parts were sound.'

From *Dublin* soon to *London* spread,
'Tis told at court, ' The Dean is dead.'
And Lady *Suffolk* in the spleen
Runs laughing up to tell the Queen.
The Queen, so gracious, mild, and good,
Cries ' Is he gone ! 'tis time he should.
' He's dead, you say ; then let him rot ;
' I'm glad the medals were forgot.
' I promis'd him, I own ; but when ?
' I only was the Princess then :
' But now, as Consort of the king,
' You know, 'tis quite another thing ' . . .

Now *Curll* his shop from rubbish drains :
Three genuine tomes of *Swift's* remains !
And then, to make them pass the glibber,

46

Revis'd by *Tibbalds*, *Moore*, and *Cibber*.
He'll treat me as he does my betters,
Publish my Will, my Life, my Letters ;
Revive the libels born to die ;
Which *Pope* must bear, as well as I.

Here shift the scene, to represent
How those I love my death lament.
Poor *Pope* will grieve a month, and *Gay*
A week, and Arbuthnot a day.

St. John himself will scarce forbear
To bite his pen, and drop a tear.
The rest will give a shrug, and cry,
' I'm sorry, but we all must die ! '

Indifference, clad in Wisdom's guise,
All fortitude of mind supplies :
For how can stony bowels melt
In those who never pity felt !
When we are lash'd, they kiss the rod,
Resigning to the will of God.

The fools, my juniors by a year,
Are tortur'd with suspense and fear ;
Who wisely thought my age a screen,
When death approach'd, to stand between :
The screen remov'd, their hearts are trembling ;
They mourn for me without dissembling.

My female friends, whose tender hearts
Have better learn'd to act their parts,
Receive the news in doleful dumps :
' The Dean is dead : (Pray what is trumps ?)
' Then, Lord have mercy on his soul !
' (Ladies, I'll venture for the vole.)
' Six deans, they say, must bear the pall :

' (I wish I knew what king to call)
' Madam, your husband will attend
' The funeral of so good a friend.
' No, madam, 'tis a shocking sight ;
' And he's engag'd to-morrow night :
' My lady Club will take it ill,
' If he should fail her at quadrille.
' He lov'd the Dean (I lead a heart)
' But dearest friends, they say, must part.
' His time was come ; he ran his race ;
' We hope he's in a better place.'

Why do we grieve that friends should die ?
No loss more easy to supply.
One year is past ; a different scene !
No farther mention of the Dean ;
Who now, alas, no more is miss'd,
Than if he never did exist.
Where's now the favourite of *Apollo* ?
Departed :—*And his Works must follow* :
Must undergo the common fate ;
His kind of wit is out of date.

Some country squire to *Lintot* goes,
Inquires for *Swift* in verse and prose.
Says *Lintot*, ' I have heard the name ;
' He died a year ago.'—' The same.'
He searches all the shop in vain.
' Sir, you may find them in *Duck Lane* :
' I sent them, with a load of books,
' Last Monday to the pastry-cook's.
' To fancy, they could live a year !
' I find you're but a stranger here.
' The Dean was famous in his time,

' And had a kind of knack at rhyme.
' His way of writing now is past :
' The town has got a better taste.
' I keep no antiquated stuff,
' But spick and span I have enough.
' Pray, do but give me leave to shew 'em :
' Here's *Colley Cibber's* birthday poem.

. . . . .

   Suppose me dead ; and then suppose
A club assembled at the Rose ;
Where, from Discourse of this and that,
I grow the Subject of their Chat.
And while they toss my name about,
With favour some, and some without ;
One, quite indifferent in the cause,
My character impartial draws :
' The Dean, if we believe report,
' Was never ill-received at court.
' As for his works in verse and prose,
' I own myself no judge of those :
' Nor can I tell what criticks thought 'em ;
' But this I know, all people bought 'em :
' As with a moral view design'd
' To cure the vices of mankind :
' His vein, ironically grave,
' Expos'd the fool, and lash'd the knave ;
' To steal a hint was never known,
' But what he writ was all his own.
   ' He never thought an honour done him,
' Because a duke was proud to own him ;
' Would rather slip aside, and choose

   the Rose] a tavern adjoining Drury Lane Theatre.

' To talk with wits in dirty shoes ;
' Despis'd the fools with stars and garters,
' So often seen caressing *Chartres*.
' He never courted men in station,
' Nor persons held in admiration ;
' Of no man's greatness was afraid,
' Because he sought for no man's aid.
' Though trusted long in great affairs,
' He gave himself no haughty airs :
' Without regarding private ends,
' Spent all his credit for his friends :
' And only chose the wise and good ;
' No flatterers ; no allies in blood :
' But succour'd virtue in distress,
' And seldom fail'd of good success ;
' As numbers in their hearts must own,
' Who, but for him, had been unknown.
    ' He kept with princes due decorum ;
' Yet never stood in awe before 'em.
' He follow'd *David's* lesson just,
' In princes never put thy trust :
' And, would you make him truly sour,
' Provoke him with a slave in power.
' The Irish senate if you nam'd,
' With what impatience he declaim'd !
' Fair LIBERTY was all his cry ;
' For her he stood prepar'd to die ;
' For her he boldly stood alone
' For her he oft' expos'd his own.
' Two kingdoms, just as faction led,
' Had set a price upon his head ;
' But not a traitor could be found,

' To sell him for six hundred pound.
  ' Had he but spar'd his tongue and pen,
' He might have rose like other men :
' But power was never in his thought,
' And wealth he valu'd not a groat :
' Ingratitude he often found,
' And pitied those who meant the wound :
' But kept the tenour of his mind,
' To merit well of humankind :
' Nor make a sacrifice of those
' Who still were true, to please his foes.
' He labour'd many a fruitless hour,
' To reconcile his friends in power ;
' Saw mischief by a faction brewing,
' While they pursu'd each other's ruin.
' But finding vain was all his care,
' He left the court in mere despair.
  ' And, oh ! how short are human schemes !
' Here ended all our golden dreams.
' What *St. John's* skill in state affairs,
' What *Ormond's* valour, *Oxford's* cares,
' To save their sinking country lent,
' Was all destroy'd by one event.
' Too soon that precious life was ended,
' On which alone our weal depended.

    .   .   .   .   .

  ' Perhaps I may allow the Dean
' Had too much satire in his vein ;
' And seem'd determin'd not to starve it,
' Because no age could more deserve it.
' Yet malice never was his aim ;
' He lash'd the vice, but spar'd the name.

' No individual could resent,
' Where thousands equally were **meant** ;
' His satire points at no defect,
' But what all mortals may correct ;
' For he abhorr'd that senseless tribe
' Who call it humour when they gibe :
' He spar'd a hump, or crooked nose,
' Whose owners set not up for beaux.
' True genuine dulness mov'd his pity,
' Unless it offer'd to be witty.
' Those who their ignorance confest,
' He ne'er offended with a jest ;
' But laugh'd to hear an idiot quote
' A verse from *Horace* learn'd by rote.
' He knew a hundred pleasing stories,
' With all the turns of Whigs and Tories :
' Was cheerful to his dying day ;
' And friends would let him have his way.
' He gave the little wealth he had
' To build a house for fools and mad ;
' And shewed, by one satirick touch,
' No nation wanted it so much.
' That kingdom he hath left his debtor,
' I wish it soon may have a better.'

(*Faulkner's Text*)
VERSES ON THE DEATH OF DOCTOR SWIFT.

WILLIAM CONGREVE

1670–1729

Fair Amoret

FAIR *Amoret* is gone astray ;
  Pursue and seek her, ev'ry Lover ;
I'll tell the Signs, by which you may
  The wand'ring Shepherdess discover.

Coquet and Coy at once her Air,
  Both study'd, tho' both seem neglected ;
Careless she is with artful Care,
  Affecting to seem unaffected.

With Skill her Eyes dart ev'ry Glance,
  Yet change so soon you'd ne'er suspect 'em ;
For she'd persuade they wound by chance,
  Tho' certain Aim and Art direct 'em.

She likes her self, yet others hates
  For that which in her self she prizes ;
And while she Laughs at them, forgets
  She is the Thing that she despises.

POETICAL MISCELLANIES, V.

Song

FALSE though she be to me and Love,
  I'll ne'er pursue Revenge ;
For still the Charmer I approve,
  Tho' I deplore her Change.

53

WILLIAM CONGREVE

In Hours of Bliss we oft have met,
　　They could not always last ;
And though the present I regret,
　　I'm grateful for the past.

WORKS, III.

The Golden Age

COME, see thy Friend, retir'd without Regret,
Forgetting Care, or striving to forget ;
In easy Contemplation soothing Time
With Morals much, and now and then with Rhime,
Not so robust in Body, as in Mind,
And always undejected, tho' declin'd ;
Not wond'ring at the World's new wicked Ways,
Compar'd with those of our Fore-fathers Days,
For Virtue now is neither more nor less,
And Vice is only vary'd in the Dress :
Believe it, *Men* have ever been the *same*,
And *Ovid's* GOLDEN AGE, is but a *Dream*.

OF IMPROVING THE PRESENT TIME.

JOSEPH ADDISON
1672–1719

Ode

THE Spacious Firmament on high,
With all the blue Etherial Sky,
And spangled Heav'ns, a Shining Frame,
Their great Original proclaim :

JOSEPH ADDISON

Th' unwearied Sun, from Day to Day,
Does his Creator's Power display,
And publishes to every Land
The Work of an Almighty Hand.

Soon as the Evening Shades prevail,
The Moon takes up the wondrous Tale,
And nightly to the listning Earth
Repeats the Story of her Birth :
Whilst all the Stars that round her burn,
And all the Planets in their turn,
Confirm the Tidings as they rowl,
And spread the Truth from Pole to Pole.

What though, in solemn Silence, all
Move round the dark terrestrial Ball ?
What tho' nor real Voice nor Sound
Amid their radiant Orbs be found ?
In Reason's Ear they all rejoice,
And utter forth a glorious Voice,
For ever singing, as they shine,
' The Hand that made us is Divine.'

THE SPECTATOR.

AMBROSE PHILIPS
1675–1749

A Winter-Piece
To the Earl of Dorset

COPENHAGEN, *March* 9, 1709

FROM Frozen Climes, and Endless Tracks of Snow,
From Streams that Northern Winds forbid to flow ;

AMBROSE PHILIPS

What Present shall the Muse to *Dorset* bring ;
Or how, so near the Pole, attempt to sing ?
The hoary Winter here conceals from Sight
All pleasing Objects that to Verse invite.
The Hills and Dales, and the Delightful Woods,
The Flowry Plains, and Silver Streaming Floods,
By Snow disguis'd, in bright Confusion lye,
And with one dazling Waste fatigue the Eye.
    No gentle breathing Breeze prepares the Spring,
No Birds within the Desert Region sing.
The Ships unmov'd the boist'rous Winds defy,
While rattling Chariots o'er the Ocean fly.
The vast *Leviathan* wants Room to play,
And spout his Waters in the Face of Day.
The starving Wolves along the main Sea prowl,
And to the Moon in Icy Valleys howl.
For many a shining League the level Main
Here spreads it self into a Glassy Plain :
There solid Billows of enormous Size,
Alpes of green Ice, in wild Disorder rise.
    And yet but lately have I seen, e'en here,
The Winter in a lovely Dress appear.
E'er yet the Clouds let fall the treasur'd Snow,
Or Winds begun thro' hazy Skies to blow.
At Ev'ning a keen Eastern Breeze arose ;
And the descending Rain unsullied froze.
Soon as the silent Shades of Night withdrew,
The ruddy Morn disclos'd at once to View
The Face of Nature in a rich Disguise,
And brighten'd ev'ry Object to my Eyes.
For ev'ry Shrub, and ev'ry Blade of Grass,
And ev'ry pointed Thorn, seem'd wrought in Glass.

AMBROSE PHILIPS

In Pearls and Rubies rich the Hawthorns show,
While thro' the Ice the Crimson Berries glow.
The thick-sprung Reeds the watry Marshes yield,
Seem polish'd Lances in a hostile Field.
The Stag in limpid Currents with Surprize
Sees Chrystal Branches on his Forehead rise.
The spreading Oak, the Beech, and tow'ring Pine,
Glaz'd over, in the freezing Æther shine.
The frighted Birds the rattling Branches shun,
That wave and glitter in the distant Sun.
   When if a sudden Gust of Wind arise,
The brittle Forrest into Atoms flies :
The crackling Wood beneath the Tempest bends,
And in a spangled Show'r the Prospect ends.
Or if a Southern Gale the Region warm,
And by Degrees unbind the Wintry Charm ;
The Traveller a miry Country sees,
And Journeys sad beneath the dropping Trees.
   Like some deluded Peasant, *Merlin* leads
Thro' fragrant Bow'rs, and thro' delicious Meads ;
While here inchanted Gardens to him rise,
And airy Fabricks there attract his Eyes,
His wand'ring Feet the Magick Paths pursue ;
And while he thinks the fair Illusion true,
The trackless Scenes disperse in fluid Air,
And Woods and Wilds, and thorny Ways appear :
A tedious Road the weary Wretch returns,
And, as He goes, the transient Vision mourns.

THE TATLER, MAY 5–7, 1709.

WILLIAM SOMERVILE

1675–1742

On presenting to a Lady a White Rose and a Red on the Tenth of June

IF this pale Rose offend your Sight,
  It in your Bosom wear ;
'Twill blush to find itself less white,
  And turn *Lancastrian* there.

But, *Celia*, should the Red be chose,
  With gay Vermilion bright ;
'Twould sicken at each Blush that glows,
  And in Despair turn White.

Let Politicians idly prate,
  Their *Babels* build in vain ;
As uncontrolable as Fate,
  Imperial Love shall reign.

Each haughty Faction shall obey,
  And Whigs, and Tories join,
Submit to your Despotick Sway,
  Confess your Right Divine.

Yet this (my gracious Monarch) own,
  They're Tyrants that oppress ;
'Tis Mercy must support your Throne,
  And 'tis like Heav'n to Bless.

OCCASIONAL POEMS.

58

JOHN PHILIPS

1676–1709

The Thirsty Poet

So pass my Days. But when Nocturnal Shades
This World invelop, and th' inclement Air
Persuades Men to repel benumming Frosts
With pleasant Wines, and crackling Blaze of Wood ;
Me lonely sitting, nor the glimmering Light
Of Make-weight Candle, nor the joyous Talk
Of loving Friend delights ; distress'd, forlorn,
Amidst the Horrors of the tedious Night,
Darkling I sigh, and feed with dismal Thoughts
My anxious Mind ; or sometimes mournful Verse
Indite, and sing of Groves and Myrtle Shades,
Or desperate Lady near a purling Stream,
Or Lover pendent on a Willow-Tree :
Mean while, I labour with eternal Drought,
And restless wish, and rave ; my parched Throat
Finds no Relief, nor heavy Eyes Repose :
But if a Slumber haply does invade
My weary Limbs, my Fancy, still awake,
Thoughtful of Drink, and eager, in a Dream
Tipples imaginary Pots of Ale :
In vain ; awake I find the settled Thirst
Still gnawing, and the pleasant Phantom curse,
  Thus do I live from Pleasure quite debarr'd.
Nor taste the Fruits that the Sun's genial Rays
Mature, *John-Apple*, nor the downy *Peach*,
Nor *Walnut* in rough-furrow'd Coat secure,
Nor *Medlar*, Fruit delicious in Decay.

59

ABEL EVANS

1679–1737

On Sir John Vanbrugh

An Epigrammatical Epitaph

UNDER this stone, Reader, survey
Dead Sir John Vanbrugh's house of clay.
Lie heavy on him, Earth ! for he
Laid many heavy loads on thee !

HACKETT'S EPITAPHS, I.

DAVID LEWIS

1683?–1760

None shall Rail

WHILE Malice, *Pope*, denies thy Page
   It's own celestial Fire ;
While Critics, and while Bards in Rage
   Admiring, won't admire ;

While wayward Pens thy Worth assail,
   And envious Tongues decry,
These Times tho' many a Friend bewail,
   These Times bewail not I.

But when the World's loud praise is thine,
   And Spleen no more shall blame,
When with thy *Homer* Thou shalt shine
   In one establish'd Fame,

DAVID LEWIS

When none shall rail, and ev'ry Lay
  Devote a Wreath to Thee ;
That Day (for come it will) that Day
  Shall I lament to see.

PIECES PUBLISH'D ON OCCASION
OF THE DUNCIAD.

EDWARD YOUNG

1683–1765

Characters of Women

(1)

THE *languid* lady next appears in state,
Who was not born to carry her own weight ;
She lolls, reels, staggers, 'till some foreign aid
To her own stature lifts the feeble maid.
Then, if ordain'd to so *severe* a doom,
She, by just stages, *journeys* round the room :
But knowing her own weakness, she despairs
To scale the *Alps*—that is, ascend the *stairs*.
My fan ! let others say who laugh at toil ;
Fan ! hood ! glove ! scarf ! is her *laconick* style.
And that is spoke with such a dying fall,
That *Betty* rather *sees*, than *hears* the call :
The motion of her lips, and meaning eye
Piece out the Idea her faint words deny.
O listen with attention most profound !
Her voice is but the shadow of a sound.
And help ! O help ! her spirits are so dead,
One hand scarce lifts the other to her head.

If, there, a stubborn pin it triumphs o'er,
She pants ! she sinks away ! and is no more.
Let the robust, and the gygantick *carve*,
Life is not worth so much, she'd rather *starve* ;
But *chew* she must herself, ah cruel fate !
That *Rosalinda* can't by *proxy* eat.

(2)

Thalestris triumphs in a manly mein,
Loud in her accent, and her phrase obscene.
In fair and open dealing where's the shame ?
What nature dares to *give*, she dares to *name*.
This *honest fellow* is sincere, and plain,
And justly gives the jealous husband pain.
(Vain is the task to Petticoats assign'd,
If wanton language shews a *naked* mind.)
And now and then, to grace her eloquence,
An oath supplies the vacancys of sense.
Hark ! the shrill notes transpierce the yielding air,
And teach the neighb'ring ecchos how to swear.
By *Jove*, is faint, and for the simple swain ;
She, on the christian System, is prophane.
But tho' the volly rattles in your ear,
Believe her *dress*, she's not a granadeer.
If thunder's awful, how much more our dread,
When *Jove* deputes a Lady in his stead ?
A *Lady* ! pardon my mistaken pen,
A shameless woman is the worst of *Men*.

EDWARD YOUNG

(3)

Few to good-breeding make a just pretence,
Good-breeding is the blossom of good sense ;
The last result of an accomplisht mind,
With outward grace, the *body's virtue*, join'd.
A violated decency, now, reigns ;
And Nymphs for *failings* take peculiar pains.
With *Indian* painters modern *toasts* agree,
The point they aim at is *deformity* :
They *throw* their persons with a hoydon-air
Across the room, and *toss* into the chair.
So far their commerce with mankind is gone,
They, for our manners, have exchang'd their own.
The modest look, the castigated grace,
The gentle movement, and slow-measur'd pace,
For which her lovers *dy'd*, her parents *pay'd*,
Are indecorums with the *modern* maid.
Stiff forms are bad, but let not worse intrude,
Nor conquer *art*, and *nature*, to be rude.

LOVE OF FAME, SATIRE V, 1725.

The Art of Life

No Man e'er found a *happy Life* by Chance,
Or yawn'd it into Being, with a Wish ;
Or, with the Snout of grov'ling *Appetite*,
E'er smelt it out, and grubb'd it from the Dirt ;
An *Art* it is, and must be learnt ; and learnt
With unremitting Effort, or be lost ;
And leave us perfect Blockheads, in our Bliss :

EDWARD YOUNG

The Clouds may drop down Titles, and Estates ;
Wealth may seek Us ; but *Wisdom* must be Sought ;
Sought before All ; but (how unlike All else
We seek on Earth ?) 'tis never sought in vain.

NIGHT THOUGHTS, VIII.

GEORGE BERKELEY, BISHOP OF CLOYNE

1685–1753

Verses on the Prospect of planting Arts and Learning in America

THE Muse, disgusted at an age and clime
  Barren of every glorious theme,
In distant lands now waits a better time,
  Producing subjects worthy fame :

In happy climes, where from the genial sun
  And virgin earth such scenes ensue.
The force of art by nature seems outdone,
  And fancied beauties by the true :

In happy climes the seat of innocence,
  Where nature guides and virtue rules,
Where men shall not impose for truth and sense,
  The pedantry of courts and schools :

There shall be sung another golden age,
  The rise of empire and of arts,
The good and great inspiring epic rage,
  The wisest heads and noblest hearts.

64

GEORGE BERKELEY

Not such as Europe breeds in her decay ;
  Such as she bred when fresh and young,
When heav'nly flame did animate her clay,
  By future poets shall be sung.

Westward the course of empire takes its way ;
  The four first acts already past,
A fifth shall close the drama with the day ;
  Time's noblest offspring is the last.

DODSLEY'S COLLECTION, VI, 1758.

JOHN GAY

1685–1732

Fishing

MARK well the various seasons of the year,
How the succeeding insect race appear ;
In this revolving moon one colour reigns,
Which in the next the fickle trout disdains.
Oft' have I seen a skilful angler try
The various colours of the treach'rous fly ;
When he with fruitless pain hath skim'd the brook,
And the coy fish rejects the skipping hook,
He shakes the boughs that on the margin grow,
Which o'er the stream a waving forrest throw ;
When if an insect fall (his certain guide)
He gently takes him from the whirling tide ;
Examines well his form with curious eyes,
His gaudy vest, his wings, his horns and size.
Then round his hook the chosen fur he winds,
And on the back a speckled feather binds,

So just the colours shine thro' ev'ry part,
That nature seems to live again in art.
Let not thy wary step advance too near,
While all thy hope hangs on a single hair;
The new-form'd insect on the water moves,
The speckled trout the curious snare approves;
Upon the curling surface let it glide,
With nat'ral motion from thy hand supply'd,
Against the stream now gently let it play,
Now in their rapid eddy roll away.
The scaly shoals float by, and seiz'd with fear
Behold their fellows tost in thinner air;
But soon they leap, and catch the swimming bait,
Plunge on the hook, and share an equal fate.

RURAL SPORTS.

Blouzelinda's Funeral

To show their love, the neighbours far and near,
Follow'd with wistful look the damsel's bier.
Sprigg'd rosemary the lads and lasses bore,
While dismally the Parson walk'd before.
Upon her grave the rosemary they threw,
The daisie, butter-flow'r and endive blue.

After the good man warn'd us from his text,
That none cou'd tell whose turn would be the next;
He said, that heav'n would take her soul, no doubt,
And spoke the hour-glass in her praise—quite out.

To her sweet mem'ry flow'ry garlands strung,
O'er her now empty seat aloft were hung.

66

With wicker rods we fenc'd her tomb around,
To ward from man and beast the hallow'd ground,
Lest her new grave the Parson's cattle raze,
For both his horse and cow the church-yard graze.
  Now we trudg'd homeward to her mother's farm,
To drink new cyder mull'd, with ginger warm.
For gaffer *Tread-well* told us by the by,
Excessive sorrow is exceeding dry.
  While bulls bear horns upon their curled brow,
Or lasses with soft stroakings milk the cow ;
While padling ducks the standing lake desire,
Or batt'ning hogs roll in the sinking mire ;
While moles the crumbled earth in hillocks raise,
So long shall swains tell *Blouzelinda's* praise.
  Thus wail'd the louts in melancholy strain,
'Till bonny *Susan* sped a-cross the plain ;
They seiz'd the lass in apron clean array'd,
And to the ale-house forc'd the willing maid ;
In ale and kisses they forget their cares,
And *Susan Blouzelinda's* loss repairs.

THE SHEPHERD'S WEEK, FRIDAY.

Sweet William's Farewell to Black-Ey'd Susan

ALL in the *Downs* the fleet was moor'd,
  The streamers waving in the wind,
When black-ey'd *Susan* came aboard.
  Oh ! where shall I my true love find !
Tell me, ye jovial sailors, tell me true,
If my sweet *William* sails among the crew.

67

William, who high upon the yard,
 Rock'd with the billow to and fro,
Soon as her well-known voice he heard,
 He sigh'd, and cast his eyes below :
The cord slides swiftly through his glowing hands
And, (quick as lightning,) on the deck he stands.

So the sweet lark, high-pois'd in air,
 Shuts close his pinions to his breast,
(If, chance, his mate's shrill call he hear)
 And drops at once into her nest,
The noblest Captain in the *British* fleet,
Might envy *William's* lip those kisses sweet.

O *Susan, Susan*, lovely dear,
 My vows shall ever true remain ;
Let me kiss off that falling tear,
 We only part to meet again.
Change, as ye list, ye winds ; my heart shall be
The faithful compass that still points to thee.

Believe not what the landmen say,
 Who tempt with doubts thy constant mind :
They'll tell thee, sailors, when away,
 In ev'ry port a mistress find.
Yes, yes, believe them when they tell thee so,
For thou art present wheresoe'er I go.

If to far *India's* coast we sail,
 Thy eyes are seen in di'monds bright,
Thy breath is *Africk's* spicy gale,
 Thy skin is ivory, so white.

Thus ev'ry beauteous object that I view,
Wakes in my soul some charm of lovely *Sue*.

Though battel call me from thy arms,
    Let not my pretty *Susan* mourn ;
Though cannons roar, yet safe from harms,
    William shall to his Dear return.
Love turns aside the balls that round me fly,
Lest precious tears should drop from *Susan's* eye.

The boatswain gave the dreadful word,
    The sails their swelling bosom spread,
No longer must she stay aboard :
    They kiss'd, she sigh'd, he hung his head.
Her less'ning boat, unwilling rows to land :
Adieu, she cries ! and wav'd her lilly hand.

SWEET WILLIAM'S FAREWELL.

Song

O RUDDIER than the Cherry,
O sweeter than the Berry,
    O Nymph more bright
    Than Moonshine Night,
Like Kidlings blith and merry.
Ripe as the melting Cluster,
No Lilly has such Lustre,
    Yet hard to tame,
    As raging Flame,
And fierce as Storms that bluster.

ACIS AND GALATEA, ACT II.

HENRY CAREY

1687(?)–1743

Love for Love's Sake

A Sonnet

I'LL range around the shady bowers,
And gather all the sweetest flowers ;
I'll strip the garden and the grave
To make a garland for my love.

When in the sultry heat of day
My thirsty nymph does panting lay,
I'll hasten to the river's brink,
And drain the floods, but she shall drink.

At night, to rest her weary head,
I'll make my love a grassy bed ;
And with green boughs I'll form a shade,
That nothing may her rest invade.

And while dissolved in sleep she lies
Myself shall never close these eyes,
But, gazing still with fond delight,
I'll watch my charmer all the night.

And then, as soon as cheerful day
Dispels the darksome shades away,
Forth to the forest I'll repair,
To seek provision for my fair.

Thus will I spend the day and night,
Still mixing labour with delight,

Regarding nothing I endure,
So I can ease for her procure.

But if the nymph whom thus I love,
To her fond swain should faithless prove,
I'll seek some dismal, distant shore,
And never think of woman more.

A Song

A HEART that 's bleeding
With deep despair,
Is ne'er succeeding
Amongst the fair.

They hate imploring,
And courtship fly ;
Each swain adoring
Is sure to die.

ALEXANDER POPE

1688–1744

Holism

ALL are but parts of one stupendous whole,
Whose body Nature is, and God the soul ;
That, chang'd thro' all, and yet in all the same ;
Great in the earth, as in th' ethereal frame ;

Warms in the sun, refreshes in the breeze,
Glows in the stars, and blossoms in the trees,
Lives thro' all life, extends thro' all extent,
Spreads undivided, operates unspent ;
Breathes in our soul, informs our mortal part,
As full, as perfect, in a hair as heart :
As full, as perfect, in vile Man that mourns,
As the rapt Seraph that adores and burns :
To him no high, no low, no great, no small ;
He fills, he bounds, connects, and equals all.
　　Cease then, nor ORDER Imperfection name :
Our proper bliss depends on what we blame.
Know thy own point : This kind, this due degree
Of blindness, weakness, Heav'n bestows on thee.
Submit.—In this, or any other sphere,
Secure to be as blest as thou canst bear :
Safe in the hand of one disposing Pow'r,
Or in the natal, or the mortal hour.
All Nature is but Art, unknown to thee ;
All Chance, Direction, which thou canst not see ;
All Discord, Harmony not understood ;
All partial Evil, universal Good :
And, spite of Pride, in erring Reason's spite,
One truth is clear, WHATEVER IS, IS RIGHT.

ESSAY ON MAN, I.

The Limits of Science

SUPERIOR beings, when of late they saw
A mortal Man unfold all Nature's law,
Admir'd such wisdom in an earthly shape,
And shew'd a NEWTON as we shew an Ape.

Could he, whose rules the rapid Comet bind,
Describe or fix one movement of his Mind?
Who saw its fires here rise, and there descend,
Explain his own beginning, or his end?
Alas what wonder! Man's superior part
Uncheck'd may rise, and climb from art to art;
But when his own great work is but begun,
What reason weaves, by Passion is undone.
   Trace Science then, with Modesty thy guide;
First strip off all her equipage of Pride;
Deduct what is but Vanity, or Dress,
Or Learning's Luxury, or Idleness;
Or tricks to shew the stretch of human brain,
Mere curious pleasure, or ingenious pain;
Expunge the whole, or lop th' excrescent parts
Of all our Vices have created Arts;
Then see how little the remaining sum,
Which serv'd the past, and must the times to come!

ESSAY ON MAN, II.

Passion and Reason

In lazy Apathy let Stoics boast
Their Virtue fix'd; 'tis fix'd as in a frost;
Contracted all, retiring to the breast;
But strength of mind is Exercise, not Rest:
The rising tempest puts in act the soul,
Parts it may ravage, but preserves the whole.
On life's vast ocean diversely we sail,
Reason the card, but Passion is the gale;

73

Nor God alone in the still calm we find,
He mounts the storm, and walks upon the wind.

ESSAY ON MAN, II.

The Mysterious Universe

LOOK round our World ; behold the chain of Love
Combining all below and all above.
See plastic Nature working to this end,
The single atoms each to other tend,
Attract, attracted to, the next in place
Form'd and impell'd its neighbour to embrace.
See Matter next, with various life endu'd,
Press to one centre still, the gen'ral Good.
See dying vegetables life sustain,
See life dissolving vegetate again :
All forms that perish other forms supply,
(By turns we catch the vital breath and die,)
Like bubbles on the sea of Matter born,
They rise, they break, and to that sea return.

ESSAY ON MAN, III.

On Love

GOD loves from Whole to Parts ; but human soul
Must rise from Individual to the Whole.
Self-love but serves the virtuous mind to wake,
As the small pebble stirs the peaceful lake ;

The centre mov'd, a circle straight succeeds,
Another still, and still another spreads ;
Friend, parent, neighbour, first it will embrace ;
His country next ; and next all human race ;
Wide and more wide, th' o'erflowings of the mind
Take ev'ry creature in, of ev'ry kind ;
Earth smiles around, with boundless bounty blest,
And Heav'n beholds its image in his breast.

ESSAY ON MAN, IV.

A little Learning

A LITTLE Learning is a dang'rous thing ;
Drink deep, or taste not the *Pierian* spring :
There shallow draughts intoxicate the brain,
And drinking largely sobers us again.
Fir'd at first sight with what the Muse imparts,
In fearless youth we tempt the heights of Arts,
While from the bounded level of our mind,
Short views we take, nor see the lengths behind ;
But more advanc'd, behold with strange surprize
New distant scenes of endless science rise !
So pleas'd at first the towr'ing *Alps* we try,
Mount o'er the vales, and seem to tread the sky,
Th' eternal snows appear already past,
And the first clouds and mountains seem the last :
But those attain'd, we tremble to survey
The growing labours of the lengthen'd way,
Th' increasing prospect tires our wandring eyes,
Hills peep o'er hills, and *Alps* on *Alps* arise !

AN ESSAY ON CRITICISM.

ALEXANDER POPE

Prisoned Souls

From the " *Elegy to the Memory of an Unfortunate Lady.*"

MOST souls, 'tis true, but peep out once an age,
Dull sullen pris'ners in the body's cage :
Dim lights of life that burn a length of years,
Useless, unseen, as lamps in sepulchres ;
Like Eastern Kings a lazy state they keep,
And close confin'd in their own palace sleep.

The Triumph of Dulness

*   *   *

IN vain, in vain,—the all-composing Hour
Resistless falls : The Muse obeys the Pow'r.
She comes ! she comes ! the sable Throne behold
Of *Night* Primæval, and of *Chaos* old !
Before her, *Fancy's* gilded clouds decay,
And all its varying Rain-bows die away.
Wit shoots in vain its momentary fires,
The meteor drops, and in a flash expires.
As one by one, at dread Medea's strain,
The sick'ning stars fade off th' ethereal plain ;
As Argus' eyes, by Hermes' wand opprest,
Clos'd one by one to everlasting rest ;
Thus at her felt approach, and secret might,
Art after *Art* goes out, and all is Night.
See skulking *Truth* to her old Cavern fled,
Mountains of Casuistry heap'd o'er her head !

Philosophy, that lean'd on Heav'n before,
Shrinks to her second cause, and is no more.
Physic of *Metaphysic* begs defence,
And *Metaphysic* calls for aid on *Sense* !
See *Mystery* to *Mathematics* fly !
In vain ! they gaze, turn giddy, rave, and die.
Religion blushing veils her sacred fires,
And unawares *Morality* expires.
Nor *public* Flame, nor *private*, dares to shine ;
Nor *human* Spark is left, nor Glimpse *divine* !
Lo ! thy dread Empire, CHAOS ! is restor'd ;
Light dies before thy uncreating word :
Thy hand, great Anarch ! lets the curtain fall ;
And Universal Darkness buries All.

THE DUNCIAD, IV.

On a Certain Lady at Court

I KNOW the thing that's most uncommon ;
  (Envy be silent and attend !)
I know a Reasonable Woman,
  Handsome and witty, yet a Friend.

Not warp'd by Passion, aw'd by Rumour,
  Not grave thro' Pride, or gay thro' Folly,
An equal Mixture of good Humour,
  And sensible soft Melancholy.

' Has she no Faults then (Envy says) Sir ? '
  Yes she has one, I must aver :

77

When all the World conspires to praise her,
The Woman's deaf, and does not hear.

MISCELLANIES, III.

Characters of Women

NOTHING so true as what you once let fall,
" Most women have no characters at all."

*　　　*　　　*

Flavia's a Wit, has too much sense to *pray* ;
To *toast* our wants and wishes, is her way ;
Nor asks of God, but of her Stars, to give
The mighty blessing, ' while we live, to live.'
Then all for Death, that Opiate of the soul !
Lucretia's dagger, *Rosamonda's* bowl.
Say, what can cause such impotence of mind ?
A Spark too fickle, or a Spouse too kind.
Wise Wretch ! with Pleasures too refin'd to please,
With too much Spirit to be e'er at ease,
With too much Quickness ever to be taught,
With too much Thinking to have common Thought :
You purchase Pain with all that Joy can give,
And die of nothing but a Rage to live.

Turn then from Wits ; and look on *Simo's* Mate,
No Ass so meek, no Ass so obstinate :
Or her, that owns her Faults, but never mends,
Because she's honest, and the best of Friends :
Or her, whose life the Church and Scandal share,
For ever in a Passion, or a Pray'r :
Or her, who laughs at Hell, but (like her Grace)
Cries, ' Oh how charming if there's no such place ! '

Or who in sweet vicissitude appears
Of Mirth and Opium, Ratafie and Tears,
The daily Anodyne, and nightly Draught,
To kill those foes to Fair ones, Time and Thought.
Woman and Fool are *two* hard things to hit ;
For true No-meaning puzzles more than Wit.
  But what are these to great *Atossa's* mind ?
Scarce once herself, by turns all Womankind !
Who, with herself, or others, from her birth
Finds all her life one warfare upon earth :
Shines in exposing Knaves, and painting Fools,
Yet is, whate'er she hates and ridicules.
No Thought advances, but her Eddy Brain
Whisks it about, and down it goes again.
Full sixty years the World has been her Trade,
The wisest Fool much Time has ever made :
From loveless youth to unrespected age,
No Passion gratify'd except her Rage.
So much the Fury still out-ran the Wit,
The Pleasure miss'd her, and the Scandal hit.
Who breaks with her, provokes Revenge from Hell,
But he's a bolder man who dares be well.
Her ev'ry turn with Violence pursu'd,
Nor more a storm her Hate than Gratitude :
To that each Passion turns, or soon or late ;
Love, if it makes her yield, must make her hate :
Superiors ? death ! and Equals ? what a curse !
But an Inferior not dependant ? worse.
Offend her, and she knows not to forgive ;
Oblige her, and she'll hate you while you live :
But die, and she'll adore you—Then the Bust
And Temple rise—then fall again to dust.

Last night, her Lord was all that's good and great ;
A Knave this morning, and his Will a Cheat.
Strange ! by the Means defeated of the Ends,
By Spirit robb'd of Pow'r, by Warmth of Friends,
By Wealth of Follow'rs ! without one distress
Sick of herself thro' very selfishness !
Atossa, curs'd with ev'ry granted pray'r,
Childless with all her Children, wants an Heir.
To Heirs unknown descends th' unguarded store,
Or wanders, Heav'n-directed, to the Poor.

  Pictures like these, dear Madam, to design,
Asks no firm hand, and no unerring line ;
Some wand'ring touches, some reflected light,
Some flying stroke, alone can hit them right :
For how should equal colours do the knack ?
Chameleons who can paint in white and black ?

  ' Yet *Cloe* sure was form'd without a spot '—
Nature in her then err'd not, but forgot.
' With ev'ry pleasing, ev'ry prudent part,
' Say, what can *Cloe* want ? '—She wants a Heart.
She speaks, behaves, and acts just as she ought ;
But never, never, reach'd one gen'rous Thought.
Virtue she finds too painful an endeavour,
Content to dwell in Decencies for ever ;
So very reasonable, so unmov'd,
As never yet to love, or to be lov'd.
She, while her Lover pants upon her breast,
Can mark the figures on an Indian chest ;
And when she sees her Friend in deep despair,
Observes how much a Chintz exceeds Mohair.
Forbid it Heav'n, a Favour or a Debt
She e'er should cancel—but she may forget.

Safe is your Secret still in *Cloe*'s ear ;
But none of *Cloe*'s shall you ever hear.
Of all her Dears she never slander'd one,
But cares not if a thousand are undone.
Would *Cloe* know if you're alive or dead ?
She bids her Footman put it in her head.
Cloe is prudent—Would you too be wise ?
Then never break your heart when *Cloe* dies.

*   *   *

But grant, in Public, Men sometimes are shown,
A Woman's seen in Private life alone :
Our bolder Talents in full light display'd,
Your Virtues open fairest in the shade.
Bred to disguise, in Publick 'tis you hide ;
There, none distinguish 'twixt your Shame or Pride,
Weakness or Delicacy ; all so nice,
That each may seem a Virtue, or a Vice.

In men, we various Ruling Passions find ;
In Women, two almost divide the kind ;
Those, only fix'd, they first or last obey,
The Love of Pleasure, and the Love of Sway.
That, Nature gives ; and where the lesson taught
Is but to please, can Pleasure seem a fault ?
Experience, this ; by Man's oppression curst,
They seek the second not to lose the first.

*   *   *

Oh ! blest with Temper, whose unclouded ray
Can make to-morrow cheerful as to-day ;
She, who can love a Sister's charms, or hear
Sighs for a Daughter with unwounded ear ;
She, who ne'er answers till a Husband cools,
Or, if she rules him, never shows she rules ;

Charms by accepting, by submitting sways,
Yet has her humour most, when she obeys ;
Let Fops or Fortune fly which way they will,
Disdains all loss of Tickets, or Codille ;
Spleen, Vapours, or Small-pox, above them all,
And Mistress of herself, tho' China fall.
  And yet, believe me, good as well as ill,
Woman's at best a Contradiction still.
Heav'n, when it strives to polish all it can
Its last best work, but forms a softer Man ;
Picks from each sex, to make the Fav'rite blest,
Your love of Pleasure, our desire of Rest ;
Blends, in exception to all gen'ral rules,
Your Taste of Follies, with our Scorn of Fools,
Reserve with Frankness, Art with Truth ally'd,
Courage with Softness, Modesty with Pride,
Fix'd Principles, with Fancy ever new ;
Shakes all together, and produces—You.

EPISTLE II *To a Lady.*

Epitaph
Intended for Sir Isaac Newton

NATURE and Nature's Law lay hid in Night :
GOD said, *Let Newton be !* and all was Light.

ALEXANDER POPE
The Proper Use of Satire

Curst be the verse, how well soe'er it flow,
That tends to make one worthy man my foe,
Give Virtue scandal, Innocence a fear,
Or from the soft-eyed Virgin steal a tear !
But he who hurts a harmless neighbour's peace,
Insults fall'n worth, or Beauty in distress,
Who lives a Lie, lame slander helps about,
Who writes a Libel, or who copies out :
That Fop, whose pride affects a patron's name,
Yet absent, wounds an author's honest fame :
Who can *your* merit *selfishly* approve,
And show the *sense* of it without the *love* ;
Who has the vanity to call you friend,
Yet wants the honour, injur'd, to defend ;
Who tells whate'er you think, whate'er you say,
And, if he lie not, must at least betray :
Who to the *Dean,* and *silver bell* can swear,
And sees at *Canons* what was never there ;
Who reads, but with a lust to misapply,
Make Satire a Lampoon, and Fiction, Lie.
A lash like mine no honest man shall dread,
But all such babbling blockheads in his stead.
     Let *Sporus* tremble—A. What ? that kind of silk,
Sporus, that mere white curd of Ass's milk ?
Satire or sense, alas ! can *Sporus* feel ?
Who breaks a butterfly upon a wheel ?
P. Yet let me flap this bug with gilded wings,
This painted child of dirt, that stinks and stings ;
Whose buzz the witty and the fair annoys,
Yet wit ne'er tastes, and beauty ne'er enjoys :

So well-bred spaniels civilly delight
In mumbling of the game they dare not bite.
Eternal smiles his emptiness betray,
As shallow streams run dimpling all the way.
Whether in florid impotence he speaks,
And, as the prompter breathes, the puppet squeaks ;
Or at the ear of *Eve*, familiar Toad,
Half froth, half venom, spits himself abroad,
In puns, or politics, or tales, or lies,
Or spite, or smut, or rhymes, or blasphemies.
His wit all see-saw, between *that* and *this*,
Now high, now low, now master up, now miss,
And he himself one vile Antithesis.
Amphibious thing ! that acting either part,
The trifling head or the corrupted heart,
Fop at the toilet, flatt'rer at the board,
Now trips a Lady, and now struts a Lord.
Eve's tempter thus the Rabbins have exprest,
A Cherub's face, a reptile all the rest ;
Beauty that shocks you, parts that none will trust ;
Wit that can creep, and pride that licks the dust.

EPISTLE TO DR. ARBUTHNOT.

Celia

CELIA, we know, is sixty-five,
Yet Celia's face is seventeen ;
Thus winter in her breast must live,
While summer in her face is seen.

How cruel Celia's fate, who hence
Our heart's devotion cannot try ;
Too pretty for our reverence,
Too ancient for our gallantry !

LADY MARY WORTLEY MONTAGU
1689–1762

The Lover : A Ballad

At length, by so much importunity press'd,
Take, C——, at once, the inside of my breast ;
This stupid indiff'rence so often you blame,
Is not owing to nature, to fear, or to shame :
I am not as cold as a virgin in lead,
Nor is Sunday's sermon so strong in my head :
I know but too well how Time flies along,
That we live but few years, and yet fewer are young.

But I hate to be cheated, and never will buy
Long years of repentance for moments of joy.
Oh ! was there a man (but where shall I find
Good sense and good nature so equally join'd ?)
Would value his pleasure, contribute to mine ;
Not meanly would boast, nor would lewdly design ;
Not over severe, yet not stupidly vain,
For I would have the power, tho' not give the pain.

No pedant, yet learned ; no rake-helly gay,
Or laughing, because he has nothing to say ;
To all my whole sex obliging and free,
Yet never be fond of any but me ;

85

LADY MARY WORTLEY MONTAGU

In public preserve the decorum that's just,
And shew in his eyes he is true to his trust;
Then rarely approach, and respectfully bow,
But not fulsomely pert, nor yet foppishly low.

But when the long hours of public are past,
And we meet with champagne and a chicken at last,
May ev'ry fond pleasure that moment endear;
Be banish'd afar both discretion and fear!
Forgetting or scorning the airs of the crowd,
He may cease to be formal, and I to be proud,
'Till lost in the joy, we confess that we live,
And he may be rude, and yet I may forgive.

And that my delight may be solidly fix'd,
Let the friend and the lover be handsomely mix'd;
In whose tender bosom my soul may confide,
Whose kindness can soothe me, whose counsel can
    guide.
From such a dear lover as here I describe,
No danger should fright me, no millions should bribe;
But till this astonishing creature I know,
As I long have liv'd chaste, I will keep myself so.

I never will share with the wanton coquet,
Or be caught by a vain affectation of wit.
The toasters and songsters may try all their art,
But never shall enter the pass of my heart.
I loath the lewd rake, the dress'd fopling despise:
Before such pursuers the nice virgin flies:
And as Ovid has sweetly in parable told,
We harden like trees, and like rivers grow cold.

SAMUEL WESLEY

1691–1739

On the Setting Up of Mr. Butler's Monument in Westminster Abbey

WHILE Butler, needy Wretch ! was yet alive,
No gen'rous Patron would a Dinner give :
See him, when starv'd to Death and turn'd to Dust,
Presented with a Monumental Bust !
The Poet's Fate is here in Emblem shown ;
He ask'd for Bread, and he receiv'd a Stone.

JOHN BYROM

1692–1763

Extempore Verses

Intended to allay the Violence of Party-Spirit

GOD bless the King, I mean the Faith's Defender ;
God bless—no Harm in blessing—the Pretender ;
But who Pretender is, or who is King,
God bless us all—that's quite another Thing.

MISCELLANEOUS POEMS.

Carefree Content

I AM Content, I do not care,
   Wag as it will the World for me ;
When Fuss and Fret was all my Fare,
   It got no ground, as I could see :

So when away my Caring went,
I counted Cost, and was Content.

With more of Thanks, and less of Thought,
   I strive to make my Matters meet ;
To seek what ancient Sages sought,
   Physic and Food, in sour and sweet :
To take what passes in good Part,
And keep the Hiccups from the Heart.

With good and gentle-humour'd Hearts
   I choose to chat where e'er I come,
Whate'er the Subject be that starts ;
   But if I get among the Glum,
I hold my Tongue to tell the Troth,
And keep my Breath to cool my Broth.

For Chance or Change, of Peace or Pain
   For Fortune's Favour, or her Frown,
For Lack or Glut, for Loss or Gain,
   I never dodge, nor up nor down :
But swing what Way the Ship shall swim,
Or tack about, with equal Trim.

I suit not where I shall not speed,
   Nor trace the Turn of ev'ry Tide ;
If simple Sense will not succeed,
   I make no Bustling, but abide :
For shining Wealth, or scaring Woe,
I force no Friend, I fear no Foe.

JOHN BYROM

Of *Ups* and *Downs*, of *Ins* and *Outs*,
   Of *they're i' th' wrong*, and *we're i' th' right*,
I shun the Rancours, and the Routs,
   And wishing well to every Wight,
Whatever Turn the Matter takes,
I deem it all but Ducks and Drakes.

With whom I feast I do not fawn,
   Nor if the Folks should flout me, faint
If wonted Welcome be withdrawn,
   I cook no Kind of a Complaint,
With none dispos'd to disagree,
But like them best, who best like me.

Not that I rate myself the Rule
   How all my Betters should behave ;
But Fame shall find me no Man's Fool,
   Nor to a Set of Men a Slave :
I love a Friendship free and frank,
And hate to hang upon a Hank.

Fond of a true and trusty Tie,
   I never loose where'er I link ;
Tho' if a Bus'ness budges by,
   I talk thereon just as I think :
My Word, my Work, my Heart, my Hand,
Still on a Side together stand.

If Names or Notions make a noise,
   Whatever Hap the Question hath,
The Point impartially I poise,
   And read, or write, but without Wrath ;

JOHN BYROM

For should I burn or break my Brains,
Pray, who will pay me for my Pains?

I love my Neighbour as myself,
  Myself like him too, by his Leave ;
Nor to his Pleasure, Pow'r, or Pelf,
  Came I to crouch, as I conceive :
Dame Nature doubtless has design'd
A Man the Monarch of his Mind.

Now taste and try this Temper, Sirs,
  Mood it, and brood it in your Breast ;
Of if ye ween, for worldly Stirs,
  That Man does right to mar his Rest,
Let me be deft, and debonair :
I am Content, I do not care.

MISCELLANEOUS POEMS.

PHILIP DORMER STANHOPE
EARL OF CHESTERFIELD

1694–1773

Advice to a Lady in Autumn

ASSES milk, half a pint, take at seven, or before ;
Then sleep for an hour or two, and no more.
At nine stretch your arms, and oh ! think when alone,
There's no pleasure in bed—MARY, bring me my
    gown :
Slip on that ere you rise ; let your caution be such,
Keep all cold from your breast, there's already too
    much.

PHILIP DORMER STANHOPE

Your pinners set right, your twitcher ty'd on,
Your prayers at an end, and your breakfast quite
    done,
Retire to some author improving and gay,
And with sense like your own, set your mind for
    the day.
At twelve you may walk, for at this time o' the year,
The sun, like your wit, is as mild as 'tis clear :
But mark in the meadows the ruin of time ;
Take the hint, and let life be improv'd in its prime.
Return not in haste, nor of dressing take heed ;
For beauty like yours, no assistance can need.
With an appetite, thus, down to dinner you sit,
Where the chief of the feast, is the flow of your wit :
Let this be indulg'd, and let laughter go round ;
As it pleases your mind, to your health 'twill redound.
After dinner two glasses at least, I approve ;
Name the first to the king, and the last to your love :
Thus cheerful with wisdom, with innocence gay,
And calm with your joys gently glide thro' the day.
The dews of the evening most carefully shun ;
Those tears of the sky for the loss of the sun.
Then in chat, or at play, with a dance, or a song,
Let the night, like the day, pass with pleasure along.
All cares, but of love, banish far from your mind ;
And those you may end, when you please to be kind.

DODSLEY'S *Collection.*

WILLIAM OLDYS

1696–1761

The Fly

An Anacreontick

Busy, curious, thirsty Fly,
Gently drink, and drink as I ;
Freely welcome to my Cup,
Could'st thou sip, and sip it up ;
Make the most of Life you may,
Life is short and wears away.

Just alike, both mine and thine,
Hasten quick to their Decline ;
Thine's a Summer, mine's no more,
Though repeated to threescore ;
Threescore Summers when they're gone,
Will appear as short as one.

THE SCARBOROUGH MISCELLANY.

JAMES THOMSON

1700–1748

The Seasons

From SPRING

Prelude

THE north-east spends his rage ; and now, shut up
Within his iron caves, the effusive south
Warms the wide air, and o'er the void of heaven
Breathes the big clouds with vernal showers distent,

At first a dusky wreath they seem to rise,
Scarce staining ether ; but by fast degrees,
In heaps on heaps, the doubling vapour sails
Along the loaded sky, and, mingling deep,
Sits on the horizon round a settled gloom :
Not such as wintry storms on mortals shed,
Oppressing life ; but lovely, gentle, kind,
And full of every hope and every joy ;
The wish of Nature. Gradual sinks the breeze
Into a perfect calm ; that not a breath
Is heard to quiver through the closing woods,
Or rustling turn the many-twinkling leaves
Of aspin tall. The uncurling floods, diffused
In glassy breadth, seem through delusive lapse
Forgetful of their course. 'Tis silence all,
And pleasing expectation.

*　　　*　　　*

Awakening

SEE, where the winding vale its lavish stores,
Irriguous, spreads. See, how the lily drinks
The latent rill, scarce oozing through the grass,
Of growth luxuriant ; or the humid bank,
In fair profusion, decks. Long let us walk,
Where the breeze blows from yon extended field
Of blossomed beans. Arabia cannot boast
A fuller gale of joy than, liberal, thence
Breathes through the sense, and takes the ravished
　　soul.
Nor is the mead unworthy of thy foot ;
Full of fresh verdure, and unnumbered flowers,

The negligence of nature, wide and wild ;
Where, undisguised by mimic art, she spreads
Unbounded beauty to the roving eye.
Here their delicious task the fervent bees,
In swarming millions, tend. Around, athwart,
Through the soft air, the busy nations fly,
Cling to the bud, and, with inserted tube,
Suck its pure essence, its ethereal soul.
And oft, with bolder wing, they, soaring, dare
The purple heath, or where the wild thyme grows,
And yellow load them with the luscious spoil.
　At length the finished garden to the view
Its vistas opens, and its alleys green.
Snatched through the verdant maze, the hurried eye
Distracted wanders ; now the bowery walk
Of covert close, where scarce a speck of day
Falls on the lengthened gloom, protracted sweeps
Now meets the bending sky, the river now
Dimpling along, the breezy ruffled lake,
The forest darkening round, the glittering spire,
The ethereal mountain, and the distant main.
But why so far excursive ? when at hand,
Along these blushing borders, bright with dew,
And in yon mingled wilderness of flowers,
Fair-handed Spring unbosoms every grace :
Throws out the snow-drop and the crocus first ;
The daisy, primrose, violet darkly blue,
And polyanthus of unnumbered dyes ;
The yellow wall-flower, stained with iron brown ;
And lavish stock that scents the garden round.
From the soft wing of vernal breezes shed,
Anemonies ; auriculas, enriched

With shining meal o'er all their velvet leaves
And full ranunculus, of glowing red.
Then comes the tulip-race, where beauty plays
Her idle freaks : from family diffused
To family, as flies the father-dust,
The varied colours run ; and, while they break
On the charmed eye, the exulting florist marks,
With secret pride, the wonders of his hand.
No gradual bloom is wanting ; from the bud,
First-born of Spring, to Summer's musky tribes :
Nor hyacinths, of purest virgin-white,
Low-bent, and blushing inward ; nor jonquils,
Of potent fragrance ; nor narcissus fair,
As o'er the fabled fountain hanging still ;
Nor broad carnations ; nor gay-spotted pinks ;
Nor, showered from every bush, the damask-rose.
Infinite numbers, delicacies, smells,
With hues on hues expression cannot paint,
The breath of Nature, and her endless bloom.

The Seasons

From SUMMER

The Sun

BUT yonder comes the powerful king of day,
Rejoicing in the east. The lessening cloud,
The kindling azure, and the mountain's brow
Illumed with fluid gold, his near approach
Betoken glad. Lo ! now apparent all,

Aslant the dew-bright earth and coloured air,
He looks in boundless majesty abroad ;
And sheds the shining day, that burnished plays
On rocks, and hills, and towers, and wandering
    streams,
High-gleaming from afar. Prime cheerer, Light !
Of all material beings first, and best !
Efflux divine ! Nature's resplendent robe !
Without whose vesting beauty all were wrapt
In unessential gloom ; and thou, O sun !
Soul of surrounding worlds ! in whom best seen
Shines out thy Maker ! may I sing of thee ?
    'Tis by thy secret, strong, attractive force,
As with a chain indissoluble bound,
Thy system rolls entire ; from the fair bourne
Of utmost Saturn, wheeling wide his round
Of thirty years, to Mercury, whose disk
Can scarce be caught by philosophic eye,
Lost in the near effulgence of thy blaze.

*   *   *

Light

THE unfruitful rock itself, impregned by thee,
In dark retirement forms the lucid stone.
The lively diamond drinks thy purest rays,
Collected light, compact ; that, polished bright,
And all its native lustre let abroad,
Dares, as it sparkles on the fair one's breast,
With vain ambition emulate her eyes.
At thee the ruby lights its deepening glow,
And with a waving radiance inward flames.

From thee the sapphire,—solid ether—takes
Its hue cerulean ; and, of evening tinct,
The purple-streaming amethyst is thine.
With thy own smile the yellow topaz burns ;
Nor deeper verdure dyes the robe of Spring,
When first she gives it to the southern gale,
Than the green emerald shows. But, all combined,
Thick through the whitening opal play thy beams ;
Or, flying several from its surface, form
A trembling variance of revolving hues,
As the sight varies in the gazer's hand.
    The very dead creation, from thy touch,
Assumes a mimic life. By thee refined,
In brighter mazes, the reluctent stream
Plays o'er the mead. The precipice abrupt,
Projecting horror on the blackened flood,
Softens at thy return. The desert joys,
Wildly, through all his melancholy bounds.
Rude ruins glitter ; and the briny deep,
Seen from some pointed promontory's top,
Far to the blue horizon's utmost verge,
Restless, reflects a floating gleam. But this,
And all the much-transported muse can sing,
Are to thy beauty, dignity, and use,
Unequal far—great delegated source
Of light, and life, and grace, and joy below !

*   *   *

The Critic

LET no presuming impious railer tax
Creative Wisdom, as if aught was formed

In vain, or not for admirable ends.
Shall little haughty ignorance pronounce
His works unwise, of which the smallest part
Exceeds the narrow vision of her mind?
As if upon a full proportioned dome,
On swelling columns heaved, the pride of art!
A critic fly, whose feeble ray scarce spreads
An inch around, with blind presumption bold,
Should dare to tax the structure of the whole.
And lives the man, whose universal eye
Has swept at once the unbounded scheme of things;
Marked their dependance so, and firm accord,
As with unfaltering accent to conclude
That this availeth nought? Has any seen
The mighty chain of beings, lessening down
From Infinite Perfection to the brink
Of dreary nothing,—desolate abyss!
From which astonished thought, recoiling, turns?
Till then, alone let zealous praise ascend,
And hymns of holy wonder, to that Power,
Whose wisdom shines as lovely on our minds,
As on our smiling eyes his servant-sun.

*   *   *

Night

AMONG the crooked lanes, on every hedge,
The glow-worm lights his gem; and through the
     dark,
A moving radiance twinkles. Evening yields
The world to night; not in her winter-robe
Of massy Stygian woof, but loose-arrayed
In mantle dun. A faint erroneous ray,

Glanced from the imperfect surfaces of things,
Flings half an image on the straining eye ;
While wavering woods, and villages, and streams,
And rocks, and mountain tops, that long retained
The ascending gleam, are all one swimming scene,
Uncertain if beheld. Sudden to heaven
Thence weary vision turns ; where, leading soft
The silent hours of love, with purest ray
Sweet Venus shines ; and from her genial rise,
When day-light sickens, till it springs afresh,
Unrivalled reigns, the fairest lamp of night.
As thus the effulgence, tremulous I drink,
With cherished gaze, the lambent lightnings shoot
Across the sky ; or horizontal dart
In wondrous shapes : by fearful murmuring crowds
Portentous deemed. Amid the radiant orbs
That more than deck, that animate the sky,
The life-infusing suns of other worlds,
Lo ! from the dread immensity of space
Returning, with accelerated course,
The rushing comet to the sun descends ;
And as he sinks below the shading earth,
With awful train projected o'er the heavens,
The guilty nations tremble. But, above
Those superstitious horrors that enslave
The fond sequacious herd, to mystic faith
And blind amazement prone, the enlightened few,
Whose godlike minds philosophy exalts,
The glorious stranger hail. They feel a joy
Divinely great ; they in their powers exult,
That wondrous force of thought, which mounting
    spurns

This dusky spot, and measures all the sky;
While, from his far excursions through the wilds
Of barren ether, faithful to his time,
They see the blazing wonder rise anew,
In seeming terror clad, but kindly bent
To work the will of all-sustaining love:
From his huge vapoury train perhaps to shake
Reviving moisture on the numerous orbs
Through which his long ellipsis winds; perhaps
To lend new fuel to declining suns,
To light up worlds, and feed the eternal fire.

With thee, serene Philosophy, with thee,
And thy bright garland, let me crown my song!
Effusive source of evidence and truth!
A lustre shedding o'er the ennobled mind,
Stronger than summer-noon; and pure as that,
Whose mild vibrations soothe the parted soul,
New to the dawning of celestial day.
Hence through her nourished powers, enlarged by
    thee,
Above the tangling mass of low desires,
That bind the fluttering crowd; and, angel-winged,
The heights of science and of virtue gains,
Where all is calm and clear; with nature round,
Or in the starry regions, or the abyss,
To reason's and to fancy's eye displayed:
The first up-tracing, from the dreary void,
The chain of causes and effects to Him,
The world-producing Essence, who alone
Possesses being; while the last receives
The whole magnificence of heaven and earth,
And every beauty, delicate or bold,

JAMES THOMSON

Obvious or more remote, with livelier sense,
Diffusive painted on the rapid mind.
  Tutored by Thee, hence Poetry exalts
Her voice of ages ; and informs the page
With music, image, sentiment, and thought,
Never to die ; the treasure of mankind,
Their highest honour, and their truest joy.

The Seasons

From AUTUMN

Storm

DEFEATING oft the labours of the year,
The sultry south collects a potent blast.
At first, the groves are scarcely seen to stir
Their trembling tops, and a still murmur runs
Along the soft-inclining fields of corn ;
But as the aërial tempest fuller swells,
And in one mighty stream, invisible,
Immense, the whole excited atmosphere
Impetuous rushes o'er the sounding world ;
Strained to the root, the stooping forest pours
A rustling shower of yet untimely leaves.
High beat, the circling mountains eddy in,
From the bare wild, the dissipated storm,
And send it in a torrent down the vale.
Exposed, and naked to its utmost rage,
Through all the sea of harvest rolling round,
The billowy plain floats wide ; nor can evade,

Though pliant to the blast, its seizing force ;
Or whirled in air, or into vacant chaff
Shook waste. And sometimes too a burst of rain,
Swept from the black horizon, broad, descends
In one continuous flood. Still over head
The mingling tempest weaves its gloom, and still
The deluge deepens ; till the fields around
Lie sunk and flatted, in the sordid wave.
Sudden the ditches swell ; the meadows swim.
Red, from the hills, innumerable streams
Tumultuous roar ; and, high above its banks,
The river lift ; before whose rushing tide
Herds, flocks, and harvests, cottages and swains
Roll mingled down.

*   *   *

Brooding

Oh ! bear me then to vast embowering shades,
To twilight groves, and visionary vales ;
To weeping grottoes, and prophetic glooms ;
Where angel forms athwart the solemn dusk,
Tremendous, sweep, or seem to sweep along ;
And voices, more than human, through the void
Deep-sounding, seize the enthusiastic ear ?
Or is this gloom too much ? Then lead, ye Powers,
That o'er the garden and the rural seat
Preside, which, shining through the cheerful hand
In countless numbers, blest Britannia sees,
Oh ! lead me to the wide extended walks,
The fair majestic paradise of Stowe.[1]

[1] The seat of Lord Viscount Cobham.

JAMES THOMSON

Not Persian Cyrus on Ionia's shore
E'er saw such sylvan scenes ; such various art
By genius fired, such ardent genius tamed
By cool judicious art ; that, in the strife,
All-beauteous Nature fears to be outdone.
And there, O Pitt ! [1] thy country's early boast,
There let me sit beneath the sheltered slopes,
Or in that temple [2] where, in future times,
Thou well shalt merit a distinguished name ;
And, with thy converse blest, catch the last smiles
Of Autumn beaming o'er the yellow woods.

The Seasons

From WINTER

Snow

THE keener tempests come ; and fuming dun
From all the livid east, or piercing north,
Thick clouds ascend ; in whose capacious womb
A vapoury deluge lies, to snow congealed.
Heavy they roll their fleecy world along ;
And the sky saddens with the gathered storm.
Through the hushed air the whitening shower
    descends,
At first thin-wavering ; till at last the flakes
Fall broad, and wide, and fast, dimming the day
With a continual flow. The cherished fields

[1] William Pitt, first Earl of Chatham.
[2] The Temple of Virtue in Stowe Gardens.

Put on their winter robe of purest white.
'Tis brightness all ; save where the new snow melts
Along the mazy current. Low, the woods
Bow their hoar head ; and, ere the languid sun,
Faint from the west, emits his evening ray,
Earth's universal face, deep-hid and chill,
Is one wild dazzling waste, that buries wide
The works of man. Drooping, the labourer-ox
Stands covered o'er with snow, and then demands
The fruit of all his toil. The fowls of heaven,
Tamed by the cruel season, crowd around
The winnowing store, and claim the little boon
Which Providence assigns them. One alone,
The redbreast, sacred to the household gods,
Wisely regardful of the embroiling sky,
In joyless fields and thorny thickets leaves
His shivering mates, and pays to trusted man
His annual visit. Half-afraid, he first
Against the window beats ; then, brisk, alights
On the warm hearth ; then, hopping o'er the
    floor,
Eyes all the smiling family askance,
And pecks, and starts, and wonders where he is.

*   *   *

Converse

Now, all amid the rigours of the year,
In the wild depth of winter, while, without,
The ceaseless winds blow ice, be my retreat
Between the groaning forest and the shore,
Beat by the boundless multitude of waves,

A rural, sheltered, solitary scene ;
Where ruddy fire and beaming tapers join
To cheer the gloom. There, studious, let me sit,
And hold high converse with the mighty dead ;
Sages of ancient time, as gods revered,
As gods beneficent, who blessed mankind
With arts and arms, and humanized a world.

*   *   *

Frost

WHAT art thou, frost ? and whence are thy keen
   stores
Derived, thou secret all-invading power,
Whom even the illusive fluid cannot fly ?
Is not thy potent energy, unseen,
Myriads of little salts, or hooked, or shaped
Like double wedges, and diffused, immense,
Through water, earth, and ether ? hence at eve,
Steamed eager from the red horizon round,
With the fierce rage of Winter deep suffused,
An icy gale, oft shifting, o'er the pool
Breathes a blue film, and in its mid career
Arrests the bickering stream. The loosened ice,
Let down the flood, and half dissolved by day,
Rustles no more ; but to the sedgy bank
Fast grows, or gathers round the pointed stone,
A crystal pavement, by the breath of heaven
Cemented firm ; till, seized from shore to shore,
The whole imprisoned river growls below.
Loud rings the frozen earth, and, hard, reflects

A double noise ; while, at his evening watch,
The village dog deters the nightly thief ;
The heifer lows ; the distant water-fall
Swells in the breeze ; and, with the hasty tread
Of traveller, the hollow-sounding plain
Shakes from afar. The full ethereal round,
Infinite worlds disclosing to the view,
Shines out intensely keen ; and, all one cope
Of starry glitter, glows from pole to pole.
From pole to pole the rigid influence falls,
Through the still night, incessant, heavy, strong,
And seizes nature fast. It freezes on ;
Till morn, late-rising o'er the drooping world,
Lifts her pale eye unjoyous. Then appears
The various labour of the silent night :
Prone from the dripping cave, and dumb cas-
    cade,
Whose idle torrents only seem to roar,
The pendent icicle ; the frost-work fair,
Where transient hues, and fancied figures rise ;
Wide-spouted o'er the hill, the frozen brook,
A livid tract, cold-gleaming on the morn ;
The forest bent beneath the plumy wave ;
And by the frost refined the whiter snow,
Incrusted hard, and sounding to the tread
Of early shepherd, as he pensive seeks
His pining flock, or from the mountain top,
Pleased with the slippery surface, swift descends.

JAMES THOMSON

From *The Castle of Indolence*

I

In lowly Dale, fast by a River's Side,
With woody Hill o'er Hill encompass'd round,
A most enchanting Wizard did abide,
Than whom a Fiend more fell is no where found.
It was, I ween, a lovely Spot of Ground ;
And there a Season atween June and May,
Half prankt with Spring, with Summer half im-
    brown'd,
A listless Climate made, where, Sooth to say,
No living Wight could work, ne cared even for Play.

II

Was nought around but Images of Rest :
Sleep-soothing Groves, and quiet Lawns between ;
And flowery Beds that slumbrous Influence kest,
From Poppies breath'd ; and Beds of pleasant
    Green,
Where never yet was creeping Creature seen.
Mean time unnumber'd glittering Streamlets
    play'd,
And hurled every-where their Waters sheen ;
That, as they bicker'd through the sunny Glade,
Though restless still themselves, a lulling Murmur
    made.

III

Join'd to the Prattle of the purling Rills,
Were heard the lowing Herds along the Vale,
And Flocks loud-beating from the distant Hills,
And vacant Shepherds piping in the Dale ;

And now and then sweet Philomel would wail,
Or Stock-Doves plain amid the Forest deep,
That drowsy rustled to the sighing Gale ;
And still a Coil the Grashopper did keep ;
Yet all these Sounds yblent inclined all to Sleep.

IV

Full in the Passage of the Vale, above,
A sable, silent, solemn Forest stood ;
Where nought but shadowy Forms were seen to
move,
As *Idless* fancy'd in her dreaming Mood.
And up the Hills, on either Side, a Wood
Of blackening Pines, ay waving to and fro,
Sent forth a sleepy Horror through the Blood ;
And where this Valley winded out, below,
The murmuring Main was heard, and scarcely heard,
to flow.

V

A pleasing Land of Drowsy-hed it was :
Of Dreams that wave before the half-shut Eye ;
And of gay Castles in the Clouds that pass,
For ever flushing round a Summer-Sky :
There eke the soft Delights, that witchingly
Instil a wanton Sweetness through the Breast,
And the calm Pleasures always hover'd nigh ;
But whate'er smack'd of Noyance, or Unrest,
Was far far off expell'd from this delicious Nest.

* * *

JAMES THOMSON

XXVIII

This Rite perform'd, All inly pleas'd and still,
Withouten Tromp, was Proclamation made.
' Ye Sons of INDOLENCE, do what you will ;
' And wander where you list, through Hall or
     Glade :
' Be no Man's Pleasure for another's staid ;
' Let Each as likes him best his Hours employ,
' And curs'd be he who minds his Neighbour's
     Trade !
' Here dwells kind Ease and unreproving Joy :
' He little merits Bliss who Others can annoy.'

XXIX

Strait of these endless Numbers, swarming round,
As thick as idle Motes in sunny Ray,
Not one eftsoons in View was to be found,
But every Man stroll'd off his own glad Way.
Wide o'er this ample Court's blank Area,
With all the Lodges that thereto pertain'd,
No living Creature could be seen to stray ;
While Solitude, and perfect Silence reign'd :
So that to think you dreamt you almost was con-
     strain'd.

XXX

As when a Shepherd of the *Hebrid-Isles*,
Plac'd far amid the melancholy Main,
(Whether it be lone Fancy him beguiles ;
Or that aërial Beings sometimes deign

To stand, embodied, to our Senses plain)
Sees on the naked Hill, or Valley low,
The whilst in Ocean *Phœbus* dips his Wain,
A vast Assembly moving to and fro :
Then all at once in Air dissolves the wondrous
Show.

*　　　*　　　*

XXXV

Here freedom reigned without the least alloy ;
Nor gossip's tale, nor ancient maiden's gall,
Nor saintly spleen durst murmur at our joy,
And with envenomed tongue our pleasures pall.
For why? there was but one great rule for all ;
To wit, that each should work his own desire,
And eat, drink, study, sleep, as it may fall,
Or melt the time in love, or wake the lyre,
And carol what, unbid, the muses might inspire.

XXXVI

The rooms with costly tapestry were hung,
Where was inwoven many a gentle tale ;
Such as of old the rural poets sung,
Or of Arcadian or Sicilian vale :
Reclining lovers, in the lonely dale,
Poured forth at large the sweetly tortured heart ;
Or, looking tender passion, swelled the gale,
And taught charmed echo to resound their smart ;
While flocks, woods, streams around, repose and
peace impart.

XXXVII

Those pleased the most, where, by a cunning hand,
Depainted was the patriarchal age ;
What time Dan Abraham left the Chaldee land,
And pastured on from verdant stage to stage,
Where fields and fountains fresh could best engage.
Toil was not then : of nothing took they heed,
But with wild beasts the silvan war to wage,
And o'er vast plains their herds and flocks to feed :
Blessed sons of nature they ! true golden age indeed !

XXXVIII

Sometimes the pencil, in cool airy halls,
Bade the gay bloom of vernal landscapes rise,
Or Autumn's varied shades imbrown the walls :
Now the black tempest strikes the astonished eyes ;
Now down the steep the flashing torrent flies ;
The trembling sun now plays o'er ocean blue,
And now rude mountains frown amid the skies ;
Whate'er Lorraine light-touched with softening hue,
Or savage Rosa dashed, or learned Poussin drew.

XXXIX

Each sound too here to languishment inclined
Lulled the weak bosom, and induced ease :
Aërial music in the warbling wind,
At distance rising oft, by small degrees,
Nearer and nearer came, till o'er the trees
It hung, and breathed such soul-dissolving airs,
As did, alas ! with soft perdition please :
Entangled deep in its enchanting snares,
The listening heart forgot all duties and all cares.

XL

A certain music, never known before,
Here lulled the pensive, melancholy mind ;
Full easily obtained. Behoves no more,
But sidelong, to the gently waving wind,
To lay the well-tuned instrument reclined ;
From which, with airy flying fingers light,
Beyond each mortal touch the most refined,
The god of winds drew sounds of deep delight :
Whence, with just cause, the harp of Æolus it hight.

XLI

Ah me ! what hand can touch the string so fine ?
Who up the lofty diapason roll
Such sweet, such sad, such solemn airs divine,
Then let them down again into the soul :
Now rising love they fanned ; now pleasing dole
They breathed, in tender musings, thro' the heart ;
And now a graver sacred strain they stole,
As when seraphic hands a hymn impart :
Wild warbling nature all ; above the reach of art !

XLII

Such the gay splendour, the luxurious state,
Of Caliphs old, who on the Tigris' shore,
In mighty Bagdat, populous and great,
Held their bright court, where was of ladies store ;
And verse, love, music, still the garland wore :
When sleep was coy, the bard, in waiting there,
Cheered the lone midnight with the muse's lore ;
Composing music bade his dreams be fair,
And music lent new gladness to the morning air.

XLIII

Near the pavilions where we slept, still ran
Soft tinkling streams, and dashing waters fell,
And sobbing breezes sighed, and oft began
(So worked the wizard) wintry storms to swell,
As heaven and earth they would together mell :
At doors and windows, threatening, seemed to call
The demons of the tempest, growling fell,
Yet the least entrance found they none at all ;
Whence sweeter grew our sleep, secure in massy hall.

XLIV

And hither Morpheus sent his kindest dreams,
Raising a world of gayer tinct and grace ;
O'er which were shadowy cast elysian gleams,
That played, in waving lights, from place to place,
And shed a roseate smile on nature's face.
Not Titian's pencil e'er could so array,
So fleece with clouds the pure ethereal space ;
Ne could it e'er such melting forms display,
As loose on flowery beds all languishingly lay.

*   *   *

XLIX

One great amusement of our household was
In a huge crystal magic globe to spy,
Still as you turned it, all things that do pass
Upon this ant-hill earth ; where constantly
Of idly busy men the restless fry

Run bustling to and fro with foolish haste,
In search of pleasures vain that from them fly,
Or which, obtained, the caitiffs dare not taste :
When nothing is enjoyed, can there be greater waste ?

L

' Of vanity the mirror,' this was called :
Here, you a muckworm of the town might see
At his dull desk, amid his ledgers stalled,
Eat up with carking care and penury ;
Most like to carcase parched on gallow-tree.
' A penny saved is a penny got.'
Firm to this scoundrel maxim keepeth he,
Ne of its rigour will he bate a jot,
Till it has quenched his fire, and banished his pot.

LI

Straight from the filth of this low grub, behold !
Comes fluttering forth a gaudy spendthrift heir,
All glossy gay, enamelled all with gold,
The silly tenant of the summer air ;
In folly lost, of nothing takes he care ;
Pimps, lawyers, stewards, harlots, flatterers vile,
And thieving tradesmen him among them share ;
His father's ghost from limbo lake, the while,
Sees this, which more damnation doth upon him
    pile.

DAVID MALLET

1705–1765

William and Margaret

'Twas at the silent, solemn hour,
  When night and morning meet ;
In glided MARGARET's grimly ghost,
  And stood at WILLIAM's feet.

Her face was like an *April* morn,
  Clad in a wintry cloud :
And clay-cold was her lilly hand,
  That held her sable shroud.

So shall the fairest face appear,
  When youth and years are flown :
Such is the robe that kings must wear,
  When death has reft their crown.

Her bloom was like the springing flower,
  That sips the silver dew ;
The rose was budded in her cheek,
  Just opening to the view.

But *Love* had, like the canker-worm,
  Consum'd her early prime :
The rose grew pale, and left her cheek ;
  She dy'd before her time.

Awake ! *she* cry'd, thy *True Love* calls,
  Come from her midnight grave ;
Now let thy *Pity* hear the maid,
  Thy *Love* refus'd to save.

DAVID MALLET

This is the dumb and dreary hour,
　When injur'd ghosts complain ;
When yauning graves give up their dead
　To haunt the faithless swain.

Bethink thee, WILLIAM, of thy fault,
　Thy pledge, and broken oath :
And give me back my maiden vow,
　And give me back my troth.

Why did you promise love to me,
　And not that promise keep ?
Why did you swear my eyes were bright
　Yet leave those eyes to weep ?

How could you say my face was fair,
　And yet that face forsake ?
How could you win my virgin heart,
　Yet leave that heart to break ?

Why did you say, my lip was sweet,
　And made the scarlet pale ?
And why did I, young, witless maid !
　Believe the flattering tale ?

That face, alas ! no more is fair ;
　Those lips no longer red :
Dark are my eyes, now clos'd in death,
　And every charm is fled.

DAVID MALLET

The hungry *worm* my *sister* is ;
  This *winding-sheet* I wear :
And cold and weary lasts our *night*,
  Till that *last morn* appear.

But hark !—the *cock* has warn'd me hence ;
  A long and late adieu !
Come, see, false *man*, how low *she* lies,
  Who dy'd for love of you.

The lark sung loud ; the morning smil'd,
  And rais'd her glistering head :
Pale WILLIAM quak'd in every limb,
  And raving left his bed.

He hy'd him to the fatal place
  Where MARGARET's body lay :
And stretch'd him on the grass-green turf,
  That wrap'd her breathless clay.

And thrice he call'd on MARGARET's name,
  And thrice he wept full sore :
Then laid his cheek to her cold grave,
  And word spake never more.

THE PLAIN DEALER.

HENRY FIELDING

1707–1754

Hunting Song

THE dusky Night rides down the Sky,
   And ushers in the Morn ;
The Hounds all join in glorious Cry,
   The Huntsman winds his Horn :
     And a Hunting we will go.

The Wife around her Husband throws
   Her Arms, and begs his Stay ;
My Dear, it rains, and hails, and snows,
   You will not hunt to-day.
     But a Hunting we will go.

A brushing Fox in yonder Wood,
   Secure to find we seek ;
For why, I carry'd sound and good
   A Cartload there last Week.
     And a Hunting we will go.

Away he goes, he flies the Rout,
   Their Steeds all spur and switch ;
Some are thrown in, and some thrown out,
   And some thrown in the Ditch :
     But a Hunting we will go.

At length his Strength to Faintness worn,
   Poor *Renard* ceases Flight ;
Then hungry, homeward we return,
   To feast away the Night :
     Then a Drinking we will go.

DON QUIXOTE IN ENGLAND.

SAMUEL JOHNSON

Slow Rises Worth

In imitation of the Third Satire of Juvenal

' HAS Heaven reserv'd, in pity to the poor,
No pathless waste, or undiscover'd shore ?
No secret island in the boundless main ?
No peaceful desert yet unclaim'd by Spain ?
Quick let us rise, the happy seats explore,
And bear oppression's insolence no more
This mournful truth is every where confess'd,
SLOW RISES WORTH, BY POVERTY DEPRESS'D :
But here more slow, where all are slaves to gold,
Where looks are merchandise, and smiles are sold ;
Where won by bribes, by flatteries implor'd,
The groom retails the favours of his lord.'

LONDON.

Happiness

In imitation of the Tenth Satire of Juvenal

WHERE then shall Hope and Fear their objects find ?
Must dull Suspense corrupt the stagnant mind ?
Must helpless man, in ignorance sedate,
Roll darkling down the torrent of his fate ?
Must no dislike alarm, no wishes rise,
No cries attempt the mercies of the skies ?
Inquirer, cease ! petitions yet remain,
Which Heav'n may hear, nor deem religion vain.

119

Still raise for good the supplicating voice,
But leave to Heav'n the measure and the choice.
Safe in His pow'r, whose eyes discern afar
The secret ambush of a specious pray'r.
Implore his aid, in his decisions rest,
Secure whate'er he gives, he gives the best.
Yet when the sense of sacred presence fires,
And strong devotion to the skies aspires,
Pour forth thy fervours for a healthful mind,
Obedient passions, and a will resign'd ;
For love, which scarce collective man can fill ;
For patience, sovereign o'er transmuted ill ;
For faith, that panting for a happier seat,
Counts death kind Nature's signal of retreat :
These goods for man the laws of Heav'n ordain,
These goods HE grants, who grants the pow'r to gain ;
With these celestial Wisdom calms the mind,
And makes the happiness she does not find.

THE VANITY OF HUMAN WISHES.

Ode : Friendship

FRIENDSHIP, peculiar boon of heaven,
   The noble mind's delight and pride,
To men and angels only given,
   To all the lower world denied.

While love, unknown among the blest,
   Parent of thousand wild desires,
The savage and the human breast
   Torments alike with raging fires.

With bright, but oft destructive gleam,
    Alike o'er all his lightnings fly,
Thy lambent glories only beam
    Around the favourites of the sky.

Thy gentle flows of guiltless joys
    On fools and villains ne'er descend ;
In vain for thee the tyrant sighs,
    And hugs a flatterer for a friend.

Directress of the brave and just,
    O guide us through life's darksome way !
And let the tortures of mistrust
    On selfish bosoms only prey.

Nor shall thine ardours cease to glow,
    When souls to peaceful climes remove ;
What rais'd our virtue here below
    Shall aid our happiness above.

The Young Author

WHEN first the peasant, long inclin'd to roam,
Forsakes his rural sports and peaceful home,
Pleas'd with the scene the smiling ocean yields,
He scorns the verdant meads and flowery fields ;
Then dances jocund o'er the watery way,
While the breeze whispers, and the streamers play :
Unbounded prospects in his bosom roll,
And future millions lift his rising soul ;

In blissful dreams he digs the golden mine,
And raptur'd sees the new-found ruby shine.
Joys insincere ! thick clouds invade the skies,
Loud roar the billows, high the waves arise ;
Sick'ning with fear, he longs to view the shore,
And vows to trust the faithless deep no more.
So the Young Author, panting after fame,
And the long honours of a lasting name,
Intrusts his happiness to human kind,
More false, more cruel, than the seas or wind.
' Toil on dull crowd,' in ecstasies he cries,
' For wealth or title, perishable prize ;
While I those transitory blessings scorn,
Secure of praise from ages yet unborn.'
This thought once form'd, all counsel comes too
    late,
He flies to press, and hurries on his fate ;
Swiftly he sees th' imagin'd laurels spread,
And feels th' unfading wreath surround his head.
Warn'd by another's fate, vain youth, be wise,
Those dreams were Settle's once and Ogilby's !
The pamphlet spreads, incessant hisses rise,
To some retreat the baffled writer flies ;
Where no sour critics snarl, no sneers molest,
Safe from the tart lampoon, and stinging jest ;
There begs of Heav'n a less-distinguish'd lot,
Glad to be hid, and proud to be forgot.

SAMUEL JOHNSON

Prologue

To Irene

YE glittering train ! whom lace and velvet bless,
Suspend the soft solicitudes of dress ;
From grovelling business and superfluous care,
Ye sons of Avarice ! a moment spare :
Votaries of Fame and worshippers of Pow'r !
Dismiss the pleasing phantoms for an hour.
Our daring bard, with spirit unconfin'd,
Spreads wide the mighty moral of mankind.
Learn here how Heav'n supports the virtuous mind,
Daring, though calm ; and vigorous, though resign'd.
Learn here what anguish racks the guilty breast,
In pow'r dependent, in success deprest.
Learn here that Peace from Innocence must flow ;
All else is empty sound, and idle show.

If truths like these with pleasing language join ;
Ennobled, yet unchang'd, if nature shine :
If no wild draught depart from reason's rules,
Nor gods his heroes, nor his lovers fools :
Intriguing wits ! his artless plot forgive ;
And spare him, beauties ! though his lovers live.

Be this at least his praise ; be this his pride ;
To force applause no modern arts are tried.
Shou'd partial cat-calls all his hopes confound,
He bids no trumpet quell the fatal sound.
Should welcome sleep relieve the weary wit,
He rolls no thunders o'er the drowsy pit.
No snares to captivate the judgement spreads ;
Nor bribes your eyes to prejudice your heads.

Unmov'd, though witlings sneer and rivals rail ;
Studious to please, yet not asham'd to fail.
He scorns the meek address, the suppliant strain,
With merit needless, and without it vain :
In Reason, Nature, Truth he dares to trust :
Ye fops be silent ! and ye wits be just !

Imitation of the Style of ****

' Hermit hoar, in solemn cell
    Wearing out life's evening grey ;
Strike thy bosom sage, and tell
    What is bliss, and which the way ! '—

Thus I spoke, and speaking sigh'd,
    Scarce repress'd the starting tear,
When the hoary sage replied,—
    ' Come, my lad, and drink some beer.'

Epigram

On George II and Colley Cibber, Esq., Poet Laureate

Augustus still survives in Maro's strain,
And Spencer's verse prolongs Eliza's reign,
Great George's acts let tuneful Cibber sing ;
For nature form'd the Poet for the King.

SAMUEL JOHNSON

On the Death of Dr. Robert Levet

CONDEMN'D to Hope's delusive mine,
　As on we toil from day to day,
By sudden blasts or slow decline,
　Our social comforts drop away.

Well tried through many a varying year,
　See Levet to the grave descend,
Officious, innocent, sincere,
　Of every friendless name the friend.

Yet still he fills affection's eye,
　Obscurely wise and coarsely kind ;
Nor, letter'd arrogance, deny
　Thy praise to merit unrefin'd.

When fainting nature call'd for aid,
　And hovering death prepar'd the blow,
His vigorous remedy display'd
　The power of art without the show.

In misery's darkest cavern known,
　His useful care was ever nigh,
Where hopeless anguish pour'd his groan,
　And lonely want retir'd to die.

No summons mock'd by chill delay,
　No petty gain disdain'd by pride ;
The modest wants of every day
　The toil of every day supply'd.

His virtues walk'd their narrow round,
   Nor made a pause, nor left a void ;
And sure the Eternal Master found
   The single talent well employ'd.

The busy day—the peaceful night,
   Unfelt, uncounted, glided by ;
His frame was firm—his powers were bright,
   Though now his *eightieth* year was nigh.

Then with no fiery, throbbing pain,
   No cold gradations of decay,
Death broke at once the vital chain,
   And forc'd his soul the nearest way.

PAUL WHITEHEAD

1710–1774

Hunting Song

THE sun from the East tips the mountains with gold ;
The meadows all spangled with dew-drops behold !
Hear ! the lark's early matin proclaims the new day,
And the Horn's chearful summons rebukes our delay.
   With the sports of the Field there's no pleasure can vye,
   While jocund we follow the Hounds in full cry.

Let the Drudge of the Town still make Riches his sport,
The Slave of the State hunt the smiles of a Court ;
No care and ambition our pastime annoy,
But innocence still gives a zest to our joy.
                    With the sports, &c.

PAUL WHITEHEAD

Mankind are all hunters in various degree ;
The Priest hunts a Living—the Lawyer a Fee,
The Doctor a Patient—the Courtier a Place,
Though often, like us, he's flung-out in the chace.
                              With the sports, &c.

The Cit hunts a Plumb—while the Soldier hunts
      Fame,
The Poet a Dinner—the Patriot a Name ;
And the practis'd Coquette, tho' she seems to refuse,
In spite of her airs, still her Lover pursues.
                              With the sports, &c.

Let the Bold and the Busy hunt Glory and Wealth ;
All the blessing we ask is the blessing of Health,
With Hound and with Horn thro' the woodlands to
      roam,
And, when tired abroad, find Contentment at home.
  With the sports of the Field there's no pleasure can vie,
  While jocund we follow our Hounds in full cry.
                    SUNG IN *Apollo and Daphne.*

WILLIAM SHENSTONE

1714–1763

Song

The Landskip

How pleas'd within my native bowers
    Erewhile I pass'd the day !
Was ever scene so deck'd with flowers ?
    Were ever flowers so gay ?

127

WILLIAM SHENSTONE

How sweetly smil'd the hill, the vale,
  And all the landskip round !
The river gliding down the dale !
  The hill with beeches crown'd !

But now, when urg'd by tender woes
  I speed to meet my dear,
That hill and stream my zeal oppose,
  And check my fond career.

No more, since DAPHNE was my theme,
  Their wonted charms I see :
That verdant hill, and silver stream,
  Divide my love and me.
                    DODSLEY'S *Collection*, v.

THOMAS GRAY

1716–1771

Sonnet

WHEN *Phoebe* form'd a wanton smile,
  My soul ! it reach'd not here !
Strange, that thy peace, thou trembler, flies
  Before a rising tear !

From midst the drops, my love is born,
  That o'er those eyelids rove :
Thus issued from a teeming wave
  The fabled queen of love.

THOMAS GRAY

Ode

On a Distant Prospect of Eton College

YE distant spires, ye antique towers,
That crown the watry glade,
Where grateful Science still adores
Her HENRY's holy Shade ;
And ye, that from the stately brow
Of WINDSOR's heights th' expanse below
Of grove, of lawn, of mead survey,
Whose turf, whose shade, whose flowers among
Wanders the hoary Thames along
His silver-winding way.

   Ah happy hills, ah pleasing shade,
Ah fields belov'd in vain,
Where once my careless childhood stray'd,
A stranger yet to pain !
I feel the gales, that from ye blow,
A momentary bliss bestow,
As waving fresh their gladsome wing,
My weary soul they seem to sooth,
And, redolent of joy and youth,
To breathe a second spring.

   Say, Father THAMES, for thou hast seen
Full many a sprightly race
Disporting on thy margent green
The paths of pleasure trace,
Who foremost now delight to cleave
With pliant arm thy glassy wave ?

The captive linnet which enthrall?
What idle progeny succeed
To chase the rolling circle's speed,
Or urge the flying ball?

   While some on earnest business bent
Their murm'ring labours ply
'Gainst graver hours, that bring constraint
To sweeten liberty:
Some bold adventurers disdain
The limits of their little reign,
And unknown regions dare descry:
Still as they run they look behind,
They hear a voice in every wind,
And snatch a fearful joy.

   Gay hope is theirs by fancy fed,
Less pleasing when possest;
The tear forgot as soon as shed,
The sunshine of the breast:
Theirs buxom health of rosy hue,
Wild wit, invention ever-new,
And lively chear of vigour born;
The thoughtless day, the easy night,
The spirits pure, the slumbers light,
That fly th' approach of morn.

   Alas, regardless of their doom,
The little victims play!
No sense have they of ills to come,
Nor care beyond to-day:
Yet see how all around 'em wait

The Ministers of human fate,
And black Misfortune's baleful train !
Ah, shew them where in ambush stand
To seize their prey the murth'rous band
Ah, tell them, they are men !

These shall the fury Passions tear,
The vulturs of the mind,
Disdainful Anger, pallid Fear,
And Shame that sculks behind ;
Or pineing Love shall waste their youth,
Or Jealousy with rankling tooth,
That inly gnaws the secret heart,
And Envy wan, and faded Care,
Grim-visag'd comfortless Despair,
And Sorrow's piercing dart.

Ambition this shall tempt to rise,
Then whirl the wretch from high,
To bitter Scorn a sacrifice,
And grinning Infamy.
The stings of Falsehood those shall try,
And hard Unkindness' alter'd eye,
That mocks the tear it forc'd to flow ;
And keen Remorse with blood defil'd ;
And moody Madness laughing wild
Amid severest woe.

Lo, in the vale of years beneath
A griesly troop are seen
The painful family of Death,
More hideous than their Queen :

This racks the joints, this fires the veins,
That every labouring sinew strains,
Those in the deeper vitals rage :
Lo, Poverty, to fill the band,
That numbs the soul with icy hand,
And slow-consuming Age.

To each his suff'rings : all are men,
Condemn'd alike to groan ;
The tender for another's pain,
Th' unfeeling for his own.
Yet ah ! why should they know their fate ?
Since sorrow never comes too late,
And happiness too swiftly flies.
Thought would destroy their paradise.
No more ; where ignorance is bliss,
'Tis folly to be wise.

Hymn to Adversity

DAUGHTER of JOVE, relentless Power,
Thou Tamer of the human breast,
Whose iron scourge and tort'ring hour,
The Bad affright, afflict the Best !
Bound in thy adamantine chain
The Proud are taught to taste of pain,
And purple Tyrants vainly groan
With pangs unfelt before, unpitied and alone.

THOMAS GRAY

When first thy Sire to send on earth
Virtue, his darling Child, design'd,
To thee he gave the heav'nly Birth,
And bad to form her infant mind.
Stern rugged Nurse ! thy rigid lore
With patience many a year she bore :
What sorrow was, thou bad'st her know,
And from her own she learn'd to melt at others' woe.

Scared at thy frown terrific, fly
Self-pleasing Folly's idle brood,
Wild Laughter, Noise, and thoughtless Joy,
And leave us leisure to be good.
Light they disperse, and with them go
The summer Friend, the flatt'ring Foe ;
By vain Prosperity received,
To her they vow their truth, and are again believed.

Wisdom in sable garb array'd
Immers'd in rapt'rous thought profound,
And Melancholy, silent maid
With leaden eye, that loves the ground,
Still on thy solemn steps attend :
Warm Charity, the gen'ral Friend,
With Justice to herself severe,
And Pity, dropping soft the sadly-pleasing tear.

Oh, gently on thy Suppliant's head,
Dread Goddess, lay thy chast'ning hand !
Not in thy Gorgon terrors clad,
Nor circled with the vengeful Band

(As by the Impious thou art seen)
With thund'ring voice, and threat'ning mien,
With screaming Horror's funeral cry,
Despair, and fell Disease, and ghastly Poverty.

Thy form benign, oh Goddess, wear,
Thy milder influence impart,
Thy philosophic Train be there
To soften, not to wound my heart.
The gen'rous spark extinct revive,
Teach me to love and to forgive,
Exact my own defects to scan,
What others are, to feel, and know myself a Man.

Ode

On the Death of a Favourite Cat Drowned in a Tub of Gold Fishes

'Twas on a lofty vase's side,
Where China's gayest art had dy'd
    The azure flowers, that blow;
Demurest of the tabby kind,
The pensive Selima reclin'd,
    Gazed on the lake below.

Her conscious tail her joy declar'd;
The fair round face, the snowy beard,
    The velvet of her paws,
Her coat, that with the tortoise vies,

Her ears of jet, and emerald eyes,
  She saw ; and purr'd applause.

Still had she gaz'd ; but 'midst the tide
Two angel forms were seen to glide,
  The Genii of the stream :
Their scaly armour's Tyrian hue
Thro' richest purple to the view
  Betray'd a golden gleam.

The hapless Nymph with wonder saw :
A whisker first and then a claw,
  With many an ardent wish,
She stretch'd in vain to reach the prize.
What female heart can gold despise ?
  What Cat's averse to fish ?

Presumptuous Maid ! with looks intent
Again she stretch'd, again she bent,
  Nor knew the gulf between.
(Malignant Fate sat by, and smil'd)
The slipp'ry verge her feet beguil'd,
  She tumbled headlong in.

Eight times emerging from the flood
She mew'd to ev'ry watry God,
  Some speedy aid to send.
No Dolphin came, no Nereid stirr'd :
Nor cruel *Tom*, nor *Susan* heard.
  A Fav'rite has no friend !

From hence, ye Beauties, undeceiv'd,
Know, one false step is n'er retriev'd,
  And be with caution bold.

Not all that tempts your wand'ring eyes
And heedless hearts, is lawful prize ;
 Nor all, that glisters, gold.
DODSLEY'S Collection, II.

The Progress of Poesy

A Pindaric Ode

I. 1

AWAKE, Æolian lyre, awake,
And give to rapture all thy trembling strings.
From Helicon's harmonious springs
A thousand rills their mazy progress take :
The laughing flowers, that round them blow,
Drink life and fragrance as they flow.
Now the rich stream of music winds along
Deep, majestic, smooth, and strong,
Thro' verdant vales, and Ceres' golden reign :
Now rowling down the steep amain,
Headlong, impetuous, see it pour :
The rocks, and nodding groves rebellow to the roar.

I. 2

Oh ! Sovereign of the willing soul,
Parent of sweet and solemn-breathing airs,
Enchanting shell ! the sullen Cares,
And frantic Passions hear thy soft controul.
On Thracia's hills the Lord of War,
Has curb'd the fury of his car,

And drop'd his thirsty lance at thy command.
Perching on the scept'red hand
Of Jove, thy magic lulls the feather'd king
With ruffled plumes, and flagging wing :
Quench'd in dark clouds of slumber lie
The terror of his beak, and light'nings of his eye.

I. 3

Thee the voice, the dance, obey,
Temper'd to thy warbled lay.
O'er Idalia's velvet-green
The rosy-crowned Loves are seen
On Cytherea's day
With antic Sports, and blue-eyed Pleasures,
Frisking light in frolic measures ;
Now pursuing, now retreating,
Now in circling troops they meet :
To brisk notes in cadence beating
Glance their many-twinkling feet.
Slow melting strains their Queen's approach declare :
Where'er she turns the Graces homage pay.
With arms sublime, that float upon the air,
In gliding state she wins her easy way :
O'er her warm cheek, and rising bosom, move
The bloom of young Desire, and purple light of Love.

II. 1

Man's feeble race what Ills await,
Labour, and Penury, the racks of Pain,
Disease, and Sorrow's weeping train,
And Death, sad refuge from the storms of Fate !

The fond complaint, my Song, disprove,
And justify the laws of Jove.
Say, has he giv'n in vain the heav'nly Muse?
Night, and all her sickly dews,
Her Spectres wan, and Birds of boding cry,
He gives to range the dreary sky:
Till down the eastern cliffs afar
Hyperion's march they spy, and glitt'ring shafts of war.

II. 2

In climes beyond the solar road,
Where shaggy forms o'er ice-built mountains roam,
The Muse has broke the twilight-gloom
To chear the shiv'ring Native's dull abode.
And oft, beneath the od'rous shade
Of Chili's boundless forests laid,
She deigns to hear the savage Youth repeat
In loose numbers wildly sweet
Their feather-cinctured Chiefs, and dusky Loves.
Her track, where'er the Goddess roves,
Glory pursue, and generous Shame,
Th' unconquerable Mind, and Freedom's holy flame.

II. 3

Woods, that wave o'er Delphi's steep,
Isles, that crown th' Egæan deep,
Fields, that cool Ilissus laves,
Or where Mæander's amber waves
In lingering Lab'rinths creep,
How do your tuneful Echos languish,
Mute, but to the voice of Anguish?

Where each old poetic Mountain
Inspiration breath'd around :
Ev'ry shade and hallow'd Fountain
Murmur'd deep a solemn sound :
Till the sad Nine in Greece's evil hour
Left their Parnassus for the Latian plains.
Alike they scorn the pomp of tyrant-Power,
And coward Vice, that revels in her chains.
When Latium had her lofty spirit lost,
They sought, oh Albion ! next thy sea-encircled coast

III. 1

Far from the sun and summer-gale,
In thy green lap was Nature's Darling laid,
What time, where lucid Avon stray'd,
To Him the mighty Mother did unveil
Her aweful face : The dauntless Child
Stretch'd forth his little arms, and smiled.
This pencil take (she said) whose colours clear
Richly paint the vernal year :
Thine too these golden keys, immortal Boy !
This can unlock the gates of Joy ;
Of Horrour that, and thrilling Fears,
Or ope the sacred source of sympathetic Tears.

III. 2

Nor second He, that rode sublime
Upon the seraph-wings of Extasy,
The secrets of th' Abyss to spy.
He pass'd the flaming bounds of Place and Time :
The living Throne, the saphire-blaze,
Where Angels tremble, while they gaze,

He saw ; but blasted with excess of light,
Closed his eyes in endless night.
Behold, where Dryden's less presumptuous car,
Wide o'er the fields of Glory bear
Two Coursers of ethereal race,
With necks in thunder cloath'd, and long-resounding
    pace.

III. 3

    Hark, his hands the lyre explore !
Bright-eyed Fancy hovering o'er
Scatters from her pictured urn
Thoughts, that breath, and words, that burn.
    But ah ! 'tis heard no more—
Oh ! Lyre divine, what daring Spirit
Wakes thee now ? tho' he inherit
Nor the pride, nor ample pinion,
That the Theban Eagle bear,
Sailing with supreme dominion
Thro' the azure deep of air :
Yet oft before his infant eyes would run
Such forms, as glitter in the Muse's ray
With orient hues, unborrow'd of the Sun :
Yet shall he mount, and keep his distant way
Beyond the limits of a vulgar fate,
Beneath the Good how far—but far above the
    Great.

THOMAS GRAY

Ode on the Pleasure arising from Vicissitude

A Fragment

Now the golden Morn aloft
  Waves her dew-bespangled wing ;
With vermeil cheek and whisper soft
  She woo's the tardy spring :
Till April starts, and calls around
The sleeping fragrance from the ground ;
And lightly o'er the living scene
Scatters his freshest, tenderest green.

New-born flocks in rustic dance
  Frisking ply their feeble feet.
Forgetful of their wintry trance
  The Birds his presence greet.
But chief the Sky-lark warbles high
His trembling thrilling ecstasy
And, less'ning from the dazzled sight,
Melts into air and liquid light.

Yesterday the sullen year
  Saw the snowy whirlwind fly ;
Mute was the musick of the air,
  The Herd stood drooping by :
Their raptures now that wildly flow,
No yesterday, nor morrow know ;
'Tis Man alone that Joy descries
With forward and reverted eyes.

Smiles on past Misfortune's brow
  Soft Reflection's hand can trace ;
And o'er the cheek of Sorrow throw
  A melancholy grace ;
While Hope prolongs our happier hour,
Or deepest shades, that dimly lour
And blacken round our weary way.
Gilds with a gleam of distant day.

Still, where rosy Pleasure leads,
  See a kindred Grief pursue ;
Behind the steps that Misery treads,
  Approaching Comfort view :
The hues of Bliss more brightly glow,
Chastised by sabler tints of woe ;
And blended form, with artful strife,
The strength and harmony of Life.

See the Wretch, that long has tost
  On the thorny bed of Pain,
At length repair his vigour lost,
  And breathe and walk again :
The meanest flowret of the vale,
The simplest note that swells the gale,
The common Sun, the air, and skies,
To him are opening Paradise.

MASON's Memoirs of Gray.

THOMAS GRAY

Satire on the Heads of Houses
Or, Never a Barrel the Better Herring

O CAMBRIDGE, attend
To the Satire I've pen'd
On the Heads of thy Houses,
Thou Seat of the Muses !

Know the Master of Jesus
Does hugely displease us ;
The Master of Maudlin
In the same dirt is dawdling ;
The Master of Sidney
Is of the same kidney ;
The Master of Trinity
To him bears affinity ;
As the Master of Keys
Is as like as two pease,
So the Master of Queen's
Is as like as two beans ;
The Master of King's
Copies them in all things ;
The Master of Catherine
Takes them all for his pattern ;
The Master of Clare
Hits them all to a hair ;
The Master of Christ
By the rest is enticed ;
But the Master of Emmanuel
Follows them like a spaniel ;

143

THOMAS GRAY

The Master of Benet
Is of the like tenet;
The Master of Pembroke
Has from them his system took;
The Master of Peter's
Has all the same features;
The Master of St. John's
Like the rest of the Dons.

P.S.—As to Trinity Hall
We say nothing at all.

HORACE WALPOLE

1717–1797

The Entail, A Fable

This piece was occasioned by the author being asked (after he had finished the little castle at Strawberry Hill and adorned it with portraits and arms of his ancestors) if he did not design to entail it on his family?

IN a fair summer's radiant morn
A BUTTERFLY, divinely born,
Whose lineage dated from the mud
Of Noah's or Deucalion's flood,
Long hov'ring round a perfum'd lawn,
By various gusts of odour drawn,
At last establish'd his repose
On the rich bosom of a rose.
The palace pleas'd the lordly guest:
What insect own'd a prouder nest?

The dewy leaves luxurious shed
Their balmy essence o'er his head,
And with their silken tap'stry fold
His limbs enthron'd on central gold.
He thinks the thorns embattled round
To guard his castle's lovely mound,
And all the bush's wide domain
Subservient to his fancied reign.

Such ample blessings swell'd the FLY !
Yet in his mind's capacious eye
He roll'd the change of mortal things,
The common fate of flies and kings.
With grief he saw how lands and honours
Are apt to slide to various owners ;
Where Mowbrays dwelt how grocers dwell,
And how cits buy what barons sell.
  " Great Phœbus, patriarch of my line,
  " Avert such shame from sons of thine !
  " To them confirm these roofs," he said ;
And then he swore an oath so dread,
The stoutest wasp that wears a sword,
Had trembled to have heard the word !
  " If law can rivet down entails,
  " These manours ne'er shall pass to snails.
  " I swear "—and then he smote his ermine—
  " These tow'rs were never built for vermine."

A CATERPILLAR grovel'd near,
A subtle slow conveyancer,
Who summon'd, waddles with his quill
To draw the haughty insect's will.

None but his heirs must own the spot,
Begotten, or to be begot :
Each leaf he binds, each bud he ties
To eggs of eggs of BUTTERFLIES.
  When lo ! how Fortune loves to teaze
Those who would dictate her decrees !
A wanton BOY was passing by ;
The wanton child beheld the FLY,
And eager ran to seize the prey ;
But too impetuous in his play,
Crush'd the proud tenant of an hour,
And swept away the MANSION-FLOW'R.

To Lady Anne Fitzpatrick, when about Five Years old, with a Present of Shells

O NYMPH, compar'd with whose young bloom
  Hebe's herself an ancient fright ;
May these gay shells find grace and room
  Both in your baby-house and sight !
Shells ! What are shells ? you ask, admiring
  With stare half pleasure half surprise ;
And fly with nature's art, enquiring
  In dear mamma's all-speaking eyes.
Shells, fairest Anne, are playthings, made
  By a brave god call'd Father Ocean,
Whose frown from pole to pole's obey'd,
  Commands the waves, and stills their motion.

From that old sire a daughter came,
  As like mamma, as blue to blue ;
And, like mamma, the sea-born dame
  An urchin bore, not unlike you.
For him fond grand-papa compels
  The floods to furnish such a state
Of corals and of cockleshells,
  Would turn a little lady's pate.
The chit has tons of bawbles more ;
  His nurs'ry 's stuff'd with doves and sparrows ;
And litter'd is its azure floor
  With painted quivers, bows, and arrows.
Spread, spread your frock ; you must be friends ;
  His toys shall fill your lap and breast :
To-day the boy this sample sends,
  —And some years hence he'll send the rest.

WORKS, IV.

WILLIAM COLLINS

1721–1759

The Manners, An Ode

Written about the time he left Oxford, 1744

FAREWELL, for clearer Ken design'd,
The dim-discov'd Tracts of Mind :
Truths which, from Action's Paths retir'd,
My silent Search in vain requir'd !
No more my Sail that Deep explores,
No more I search those magic Shores,

What Regions part the World of Soul,
Or whence thy Streams, *Opinion*, roll :
If e'er I round such Fairy Field,
Some Pow'r impart the Spear and Shield,
At which the Wizzard *Passions* fly,
By which the Giant *Follies* die !

Farewell the Porch whose Roof is seen,
Arch'd with th' enlivening Olive's Green :
Where *Science*, prank'd in tissued Vest,
By *Reason*, *Pride*, and *Fancy* drest,
Comes like a Bride so trim array'd,
To wed with *Doubt* in *Plato's* Shade !

Youth of the quick uncheated Sight,
Thy walks, *Observance*, more invite !
O thou, who lov'st that ampler Range,
Where Life's wide Prospects round thee change,
And with her mingling Sons ally'd,
Throw'st the prattling Page aside :
To me in Converse sweet impart,
To read in Man the native Heart,
To learn, where Science sure is found,
From Nature as she lives around :
And gazing oft her Mirror true,
By turns each shifting Image view !
Till meddling *Art's* officious Lore,
Reverse the Lessons taught before,
Alluring him from a safer Rule,
To dream in her enchanted School ;
Thou Heav'n, whate'er of Great we boast,
Hast blest this social Science most.

Retiring hence to thoughtful Cell,
As *Fancy* breathes her potent Spell,

Not vain she finds the charmful Task,
In Pageant quaint, in motley Mask,
Behold before her musing Eyes,
The countless *Manners* round her rise ;
While ever varying as they pass,
To some *Comtempt* applies her Glass :
With these the *white rob'd Maids* combine,
And those the laughing *Satyrs* join !
But who is He whom now she views,
In Robe of wild contending Hues ?
Thou by the Passions nurs'd, I greet
The comic Sock that binds thy Feet !
O *Humour*, Thou whose Name is known
To *Britain's* favor'd Isle alone :
Me too amidst thy Band admit,
There where the young-eyed healthful *Wit*,
(Whose Jewels in his crisped Hair
Are plac'd each other's Beams to share,
Whom no Delights from Thee divide)
In Laughter loos'd attends thy Side !
   By old *Miletus* who so long
Has ceas'd his Love-inwoven Song :
By all you taught the *Tuscan* Maids,
In chang'd *Italia's* modern Shades :
By Him, whose Knight's distinguish'd Name
Refin'd a Nation's Lust of Fame ;
Whose Tales ev'n now, with Echos sweet,
Castilia's Moorish Hills repeat :
Or Him, whom *Seine's* blue Nymphs deplore,
In watchet Weeds on *Gallia's* Shore,
Who drew the sad *Sicilian* Maid,
By Virtues in her Sire betray'd :

O Nature boon, from whom proceed
Each forceful Thought, each prompted Deed ;
If but from Thee I hope to feel,
On all my Heart imprint thy Seal !
Let some retreating Cynic find,
Those oft-turn'd Scrolls I leave behind,
The *Sports* and I this Hour agree,
To rove thy Scene-full World with Thee !

From *Odes on Several Subjects*

Ode to Simplicity

O THOU by *Nature* taught,
To breathe her genuine Thought,
In Numbers warmly pure, and sweetly strong :
Who first on Mountains wild,
In *Fancy* loveliest Child,
Thy Babe, or *Pleasure*'s, nurs'd the Pow'rs of Song !

Thou, who with Hermit Heart
Disdain'st the Wealth of Art,
And Gauds, and pageant Weeds, and trailing Pall :
But com'st a decent Maid
In *Attic* Robe array'd,
O chaste unboastful Nymph, to Thee I call !

By all the honey'd Store
On *Hybla*'s Thymy Shore,

By all her Blooms, and mingled Murmurs dear,
  By Her, whose Love-lorn Woe
  In Ev'ning Musings slow
Sooth'd sweetly sad *Electra*'s Poet's Ear !

  By old *Cephisus* deep,
  Who spread his wavy Sweep
In warbled Wand'rings round thy green Retreat,
  On whose enamel'd Side
  When holy *Freedom* died
No equal Haunt allur'd thy future Feet.

  O Sister meek of Truth,
  To my admiring Youth,
Thy sober Aid and native Charms infuse !
  The Flow'rs that sweetest breathe,
  Tho' Beauty cull'd the Wreath,
Still ask thy Hand to range their order'd Hues.

  While *Rome* could none esteem
  But Virtue's Patriot Theme,
You lov'd her Hills, and led her Laureate Band :
  But staid to sing alone
  To one distinguish'd Throne,
And turn'd thy Face, and fled her alter'd Land.

  No more, in Hall or Bow'r,
  The Passions own thy Pow'r,
Love, only Love her forceless Numbers mean :
  For Thou hast left her Shrine,
  Nor Olive more, nor Vine,
Shall gain thy Feet to bless the servile Scene.

Tho' Taste, tho' Genius bless,
  To some divine Excess,
Faints the cold Work till Thou inspire the whole;
  What each, what all supply,
  May court, may charm, our Eye,
Thou, only Thou can'st raise the meeting Soul!

  Of These let others ask,
  To aid some mighty Task,
I only seek to find thy temp'rate Vale:
  Where oft my Reed might sound
  To Maids and Shepherds round,
And all thy Sons, O *Nature*, learn my Tale.

Ode

Written in the beginning of the Year 1746

How sleep the Brave, who sink to Rest,
By all their Country's Wishes blest!
When *Spring*, with dewy Fingers cold,
Returns to deck their hallow'd Mold,
She there shall dress a sweeter Sod,
Than *Fancy*'s Feet have ever trod.

By Fairy Hands their Knell is rung,
By Forms unseen their Dirge is sung;
There *Honour* comes, a Pilgrim grey,
To bless the Turf that wraps their Clay,
And *Freedom* shall a-while repair,
To dwell a weeping Hermit there!

WILLIAM COLLINS

Ode to Evening

IF ought of oaten stop, or pastoral song,
May hope, chaste EVE, to sooth thy modest ear,
    Like thy own solemn springs,
    Thy springs, and dying gales,
O NYMPH reserv'd, while now the bright-hair'd sun
Sits in yon western tent, whose cloudy skirts,
    With brede ethereal wove,
    O'erhang his wavy bed :
Now air is hush'd, save where the weak-ey'd bat,
With short shrill shriek flits by on leathern wing,
    Or where the Beetle winds
    His small but sullen horn,
As oft he rises 'midst the twilight path,
Against the pilgrim born in heedless hum :
    Now teach me, Maid compos'd,
    To breathe some soften'd strain,
Whose numbers stealing thro' thy darkning vale,
May not unseemly with its stillness suit,
    As musing slow, I hail
    Thy genial lov'd return !
For when thy folding star arising shews
His paly circlet, at his warning lamp
    The fragrant Hours, and Elves
    Who slept in flow'rs the day,
And many a Nymph who wreaths her brows with
      sedge,
And sheds the fresh'ning dew, and lovelier still,
    The PENSIVE PLEASURES sweet
    Prepare thy shadowy car.
Then lead, calm Vot'ress, where some sheety lake

Cheers the lone heath, or some time-hallow'd pile,
 Or up-land fallows grey
 Reflect it's last cool gleam.
But when chill blust'ring winds, or driving rain,
Forbid my willing feet, be mine the hut,
 That from the mountain's side,
 Views wilds, and swelling floods,
And hamlets brown, and dim-discover'd spires,
And hears their simple bell, and marks o'er all
 Thy dewy fingers draw
 The gradual dusky veil.
While Spring shall pour his show'rs, as oft he wont,
And bathe thy breathing tresses, meekest Eve!
 While Summer loves to sport
 Beneath thy ling'ring light;
While sallow Autumn fills thy lap with leaves;
Or Winter yelling thro' the troublous air,
 Affrights thy shrinking train,
 And rudely rends thy robes;
So long, sure-found beneath the Sylvan shed,
Shall FANCY, FRIENDSHIP, SCIENCE, rose-lip'd HEALTH,
 Thy gentlest influence own,
 And hymn thy fav'rite name!

Ode on the Death of Thomson

IN yonder Grave a DRUID lies
 Where slowly winds the stealing Wave!
The *Year*'s best Sweets shall duteous rise
 To deck *it's* POET's sylvan Grave!

In yon deep Bed of whisp'ring Reeds
　　His airy Harp shall now be laid,
That He, whose Heart in Sorrow bleeds,
　　May love thro' Life the soothing Shade.

Then Maids and Youths shall linger here,
　　And while it's Sounds at distance swell,
Shall sadly seem in Pity's Ear
　　To hear the WOODLAND PILGRIM's Knell.

REMEMBRANCE oft shall haunt the Shore
　　When THAMES in Summer-wreaths is drest,
And oft suspend the dashing Oar
　　To bid his gentle Spirit rest !

And oft as EASE and HEALTH retire
　　To breezy Lawn, or Forest deep,
The Friend shall view yon whit'ning Spire,
　　And 'mid the varied Landschape weep.

But Thou, who own'st that Earthly Bed,
　　Ah ! what will ev'ry Dirge avail ?
Or Tears, which LOVE and PITY shed,
　　That mourn beneath the gliding Sail !

Yet lives there one, whose heedless Eye
　　Shall scorn thy pale Shrine glimm'ring near ?
With Him, Sweet Bard, may FANCY die,
　　And JOY desert the blooming Year.

But thou, lorn STREAM, whose sullen Tide
  No sedge-crown'd SISTERS now attend,
Now waft me from the green Hill's Side
  Whose cold Turf hides the buried FRIEND !

And see, the Fairy Valleys fade,
  Dun *Night* has veil'd the solemn View !
—Yet once again, Dear parted SHADE,
  Meek NATURE's CHILD, again adieu !

The genial Meads assign'd to bless
  Thy Life, shall mourn thy early Doom ;
Their Hinds, and Shepherd-Girls shall dress
  With simple Hands thy rural Tomb.

Long, long, thy Stone and pointed Clay
  Shall melt the musing BRITON's Eyes,
O ! VALES, and WILD WOODS, shall HE say
  In yonder Grave YOUR DRUID lies !

Dirge in Cymbeline

To fair FIDELE's grassy Tomb
  Soft Maids, and Village Hinds shall bring
Each op'ning Sweet, of earliest Bloom,
  And rifle all the breathing Spring.

No wailing Ghost shall dare appear
  To vex with Shrieks this quiet Grove :
But Shepherd Lads assemble here,
  And melting Virgins own their Love.

No wither'd Witch shall here be seen,
  No Goblins lead their Nightly crew :
The Female Fays shall haunt the Green,
  And dress thy Grave with pearly Dew !

The Redbreast oft at Ev'ning Hours
  Shall kindly lend his little Aid,
With hoary Moss, and gather'd Flow'rs,
  To deck the Ground where thou art laid.

When howling Winds, and beating Rain,
  In Tempests shake the sylvan Cell :
Or midst the Chace on ev'ry Plain,
  The tender Thought on thee shall dwell.

Each lonely Scene shall thee restore,
  For thee the Tear be duly shed :
Belov'd, till Life could charm no more ;
  And mourn'd, till Pity's self be dead.

AN EPISTLE ADDREST TO SIR THOMAS HANMER.

JOSEPH WARTON

1722–1800

The Revenge of America

WHEN fierce Pisarro's legions flew
O'er ravaged fields of rich Peru,
Struck with his bleeding people's woes,
Old India's awful Genius rose.

JOSEPH WARTON

He sat on Andes' topmost stone,
And heard a thousand nations groan ;
For grief his feathery crown he tore,
To see huge Plata foam with gore ;
He broke his arrows, stampt the ground,
To view his cities smoking round.
'What woes (he cried) hath lust of gold
O'er my poor country widely roll'd ;
Plunderers proceed ! my bowels tear,
But ye shall meet destruction there ;
From the deep-vaulted mine shall rise
Th' insatiate fiend, pale Avarice,
Whose steps shall trembling Justice fly,
Peace, Order, Law, and Amity !
I see all Europe's children curst
With lucre's universal thirst ;
The rage that sweeps my sons away,
By baneful gold shall well repay.'

OLIVER GOLDSMITH

1728–1774

An Elegy on that Glory of her Sex,
Mrs. Mary Blaize

GOOD people all, with one accord,
 Lament for Madam BLAIZE,
Who never wanted a good word—
 From those who spoke her praise.

The needy seldom pass'd her door,
  And always found her kind ;
She freely lent to all the poor,—
  Who left a pledge behind.

She strove the neighbourhood to please,
  With manners wond'rous winning,
And never follow'd wicked ways,—
  Unless when she was sinning.

At church, in silks and sattins new,
  With hoop of monstrous size,
She never slumber'd in her pew,—
  But when she shut her eyes.

Her love was sought, I do aver,
  By twenty beaus and more ;
The king himself has follow'd her,—
  When she has walk'd before.

But now her wealth and finery fled,
  Her hangers-on cut short all ;
The doctors found, when she was dead,—
  Her last disorder mortal.

Let us lament, in sorrow sore,
  For Kent-street well may say,
That had she liv'd a twelve-month more,
  She had not dy'd to-day.

OLIVER GOLDSMITH

Hope

To the last moment of his breath
  On Hope the wretch relies,
And even the pang preceding death
  Bids Expectation rise.

Hope like the gleaming taper's light
  Adorns and cheers our way,
And still as darker grows the night
  Emits a brighter ray.

THE CAPTIVITY, ACT II.

Farewell to Poetry

DEAR charming nymph, neglected and decried,
My shame in crowds, my solitary pride ;
Thou source of all my bliss, and all my woe,
That found'st me poor at first, and keep'st me so ;
Thou guide by which the nobler arts excell,
Thou nurse of every virtue, fare thee well.
Farewell, and O where'er thy voice be tried,
On Torno's cliffs, or Pambamarca's side,
Whether where equinoctial fervours glow,
Or winter wraps the polar world in snow,
Still let thy voice, prevailing over time,
Redress the rigours of the inclement clime ;
Aid slighted truth with thy persuasive strain,
Teach erring man to spurn the rage of gain ;

Teach him, that states of native strength possest,
Tho' very poor, may still be very blest ;
That trade's proud empire hastes to swift decay,
As ocean sweeps the labour'd mole away ;
While self-dependent power can time defy,
As rocks resist the billows and the sky.

THE DESERTED VILLAGE.

Edmund Burke

HERE lies our good Edmund, whose genius was such,
We scarcely can praise it, or blame it too much ;
Who, born for the Universe, narrow'd his mind,
And to party gave up, what was meant for mankind.
Tho' fraught with all learning, yet straining his throat,
To persuade Tommy Townsend to lend him a vote ;
Who, too deep for his hearers, still went on refining,
And thought of convincing, while they thought of
    dining ;
Tho' equal to all things, for all things unfit,
Too nice for a statesman, too proud for a wit :
For a patriot too cool ; for a drudge, disobedient,
And too fond of the *right* to pursue the *expedient*.
In short, 'twas his fate, unemploy'd, or in play, Sir,
To eat mutton cold, and cut blocks with a razor.

RETALIATION.

OLIVER GOLDSMITH

David Garrick

HERE lies David Garrick, describe me who can,
An abridgment of all that was pleasant in man ;
As an actor, confest without rival to shine,
As a wit, if not first, in the very first line,
Yet with talents like these, and an excellent heart,
The man had his failings, a dupe to his art ;
Like an ill judging beauty, his colours he spread,
And beplaister'd, with rouge, his own natural red.
On the stage he was natural, simple, affecting,
'Twas only that, when he was off, he was acting :
With no reason on earth to go out of his way,
He turn'd and he varied full ten times a day ;
Tho' secure of our hearts, yet confoundedly sick,
If they were not his own by finessing and trick,
He cast off his friends, as a huntsman his pack,
For he knew when he pleased he could whistle them
    back.
Of praise, a mere glutton, he swallowed what came,
And the puff of a dunce, he mistook it for fame ;
'Till his relish grown callous, almost to disease,
Who pepper'd the highest, was surest to please.
But let us be candid, and speak out our mind,
If dunces applauded, he paid them in kind.
Ye Kenricks, ye Kellys, and Woodfalls so grave,
What a commerce was yours, while you got and
    you gave ?
How did Grub-street re-echo the shouts that you
    rais'd,
While he was beroscius'd, and you were beprais'd ?

But peace to his spirit, wherever it flies,
To act as an angel, and mix with the skies :
Those poets, who owe their best fame to his skill,
Shall still be his flatterers, go where he will.
Old Shakespeare, receive him, with praise and with
    love,
And Beaumonts and Bens be his Kellys above.

RETALIATION.

Elegy on the Death of a Mad Dog

Good people all, of every sort,
  Give ear unto my Song ;
And if you find it wond'rous short.
  It cannot hold you long.

In Isling town there was a man,
  Of whom the world might say,
That still a godly race he ran,
  Whene'er he went to pray.

A kind and gentle heart he had,
  To comfort friends and foes ;
The naked every day he clad,
  When he put on his cloths.

And in that town a dog was found,
  As many dogs there be,
Both mungrel, puppy, whelp, and hound,
  And curs of low degree.

OLIVER GOLDSMITH

The dog and man at first were friends ;
  But when a pique began,
The dog, to gain his private ends,
  Went mad and bit the man.

Around from all the neighbouring streets,
  The wondering neighbours ran,
And swore the dog had lost his wits,
  To bite so good a man.

The wound it seem'd both sore and sad,
  To every christian eye ;
And while they swore the dog was mad,
  They swore the man would die.

But soon a wonder came to light,
  That shew'd the rogues they lied,
The man recovered of the bite,
  The dog it was that dy'd.

THE VICAR OF WAKEFIELD.

Song

WHEN lovely woman stoops to folly,
  And finds too late that men betray,
What charm can sooth her melancholy,
  What art can wash her guilt away ?

The only art her guilt to cover,
  To hide her shame from every eye,
To give repentance to her lover,
  And wring his bosom—is to die.

THE VICAR OF WAKEFIELD.

OLIVER GOLDSMITH

Sir Joshua Reynolds

HERE Reynolds is laid, and to tell you my mind,
He has not left a better or wiser behind ;
His pencil was striking, resistless and grand,
His manners were gentle, complying and bland ;
Still born to improve us in every part,
His pencil our faces, his manners our heart :
To coxcombs averse, yet most civilly steering,
When they judged without skill he was still hard of
     hearing :
When they talk'd of their Raphaels, Corregios and
     stuff,
He shifted his trumpet, and only took snuff.

RETALIATION.

CHARLES CHURCHILL

1731–1764

On Himself

ME, whom no muse of heav'nly birth inspires,
No judgment tempers when rash genius fires ;
Who boast no merit but mere knack of rhime,
Short gleams of sense, and satire out of time,
Who cannot follow where *trim* fancy leads
By *prattling* streams o'er *flow'r-empurpled* meads ;
Who often, but without success, have pray'd
For *apt* ALLITERATION's *artful aid* ;
Who would, but cannot, with a master's skill,
Coin fine new epithets, *which mean no ill,*

Me, thus uncouth, thus ev'ry way unfit
For *pacing* poesy, and *ambling* wit,
TASTE with contempt beholds, nor deigns to place
Amongst the lowest of her favour'd race.

THE PROPHECY OF FAMINE.

WILLIAM COWPER

1731–1800

Epitaph on " Fop "

A Dog belonging to Lady Throckmorton

THOUGH once a puppy, and though Fop by name,
Here moulders one whose bones some honour claim ;
No sycophant, although of spaniel race,
And though no hound, a martyr to the chase.
Ye squirrels, rabbits, leverets, rejoice !
Your haunts no longer echo to his voice ;
This record of his fate exulting view,
He died worn out with vain pursuit of you.
  " Yes "—the indignant shade of Fop replies—
" And worn with vain pursuit man also dies."

To a Young Lady

SWEET stream that winds through yonder glade,
Apt emblem of a virtuous maid !
Silent and chaste she steals along,
Far from the world's gay busy throng,

With gentle yet prevailing force,
Intent upon her destined course ;
Graceful and useful all she does,
Blessing and blessed where'er she goes ;
Pure-bosomed as that watery glass,
And heaven reflected in her face !

On the Loss of the " Royal George "

TOLL for the brave !
  The brave that are no more !
All sunk beneath the wave.
  Fast by their native shore !

Eight hundred of the brave,
  Whose courage well was tried,
Had made the vessel heel,
  And laid her on her side.

A land-breeze shook the shrouds,
  And she was overset ;
Down went the *Royal George*,
  With all her crew complete.

Toll for the brave !
  Brave Kempenfelt is gone ;
His last sea-fight is fought ;
  His work of glory done.

It was not in the battle ;
  No tempest gave the shock ;
She sprang no fatal leak ;
  She ran upon no rock.

His sword was in his sheath ;
  His fingers held the pen,
When Kempenfelt went down
  With twice four hundred men.

Weigh the vessel up,
  Once dreaded by our foes !
And mingle with our cup
  The tears that England owes.

Her timbers yet are sound,
  And she may float again
Full charged with England's thunder,
  And plough the distant main.

But Kempenfelt is gone,
  His victories are o'er ;
And he and his eight hundred
  Shall plough the wave no more.

The Solitude of Alexander Selkirk

I AM monarch of all I survey,
  My right there is none to dispute,
From the centre all round to the sea,
  I am lord of the fowl and the brute.

WILLIAM COWPER

O Solitude ! where are the charms
 That sages have seen in thy face ?
Better dwell in the midst of alarms,
 Than reign in this horrible place.

I am out of humanity's reach,
 I must finish my journey alone,
Never hear the sweet music of speech,
 I start at the sound of my own.
The beasts that roam over the plain,
 My form with indifference see ;
They are so unacquainted with man,
 Their tameness is shocking to me.

Society, friendship, and love,
 Divinely bestowed upon man,
Oh, had I the wings of a dove,
 How soon would I taste you again !
My sorrows I then might assuage
 In the ways of religion and truth,
Might learn from the wisdom of age,
 And be cheered by the sallies of youth.

Religion ! what treasure untold
 Resides in that heavenly word !
More precious than silver and gold,
 Or all that this earth can afford.
But the sound of the church-going bell
 These valleys and rocks never heard
Never sighed at the sound of a knell,
 Or smiled when a sabbath appeared.

WILLIAM COWPER

Ye winds, that have made me your sport,
  Convey to this desolate shore
Some cordial endearing report
  Of a land I shall visit no more.
My friends,—do they now and then send
  A wish or a thought after me?
O tell me I yet have a friend,
  Though a friend I am never to see.

How fleet is a glance of the mind!
  Compared with the speed of its flight,
The tempest itself lags behind,
  And the swift-winged arrows of light.
When I think of my own native land,
  In a moment I seem to be there;
But alas! recollection at hand
  Soon hurries me back to despair.

But the sea-fowl is gone to her nest,
  The beast is laid down in his lair,
Even here is a season of rest,
  And I to my cabin repair.
There's mercy in every place,
  And mercy, encouraging thought!
Gives even affliction a grace,
  And reconciles man to his lot.

WILLIAM COWPER

To Mrs. Unwin

MARY! I want a lyre with other strings,
Such aid from Heaven as some have feigned they
    drew,
An eloquence scarce given to mortals, new
And undebased by praise of meaner things,
That, ere through age or woe I shed my wings,
I may record thy worth with honour due,
In verse as musical as thou art true,
And that immortalizes whom it sings.
But thou hast little need. There is a book
By seraphs writ with beams of heavenly light,
On which the eyes of God not rarely look,
A chronicle of actions just and bright :
There all thy deeds, my faithful Mary, shine,
And, since thou own'st that praise, I spare thee mine.

Boadicea : An Ode

WHEN the British warrior queen,
   Bleeding from the Roman rods,
Sought, with an indignant mien,
   Counsel of her country's gods,

Sage beneath a spreading oak
   Sat the Druid, hoary chief,
Every burning word he spoke
   Full of rage and full of grief :

" Princess ! if our agèd eyes
  Weep upon thy matchless wrongs,
'Tis because resentment ties
  All the terrors of our tongues.

" Rome shall perish,—write that word
  In the blood that she has spilt ;
Perish hopeless and abhorred,
  Deep in ruin as in guilt.

" Rome, for empire far renowned,
  Tramples on a thousand states ;
Soon her pride shall kiss the ground,—
  Hark ! the Gaul is at her gates.

" Other Romans shall arise,
  Heedless of a soldier's name,
Sounds, not arms, shall win the prize,
  Harmony the path to fame.

" Then the progeny that springs
  From the forests of our land,
Armed with thunder, clad with wings,
  Shall a wider world command.

" Regions Caesar never knew
  Thy posterity shall sway,
Where his eagles never flew,
  None invincible as they."

Such the bard's prophetic words,
  Pregnant with celestial fire,

Bending as he swept the chords
　　Of his sweet but awful lyre.

She, with all a monarch's pride,
　　Felt them in her bosom glow,
Rushed to battle, fought and died,
　　Dying, hurled them at the foe.

" Ruffians, pitiless as proud,
　　Heaven awards the vengeance due ;
Empire is on us bestowed,
　　Shame and ruin wait for you ! "

Epitaph on a Hare

HERE lies, whom hound did ne'er pursue,
　　Nor swifter greyhound follow,
Whose feet ne'er tainted morning dew,
　　Nor ear heard huntsman's halloo ;

Old Tiney, surliest of his kind,
　　Who, nursed with tender care,
And to domestic bounds confined,
　　Was still a wild Jack hare,

Though duly from my hand he took
　　His pittance every night,
He did it with a jealous look,
　　And, when he could, would bite.

173

His diet was of wheaten bread,
   And milk, and oats, and straw ;
Thistles, or lettuces instead,
   With sand to scour his maw.

On twigs of hawthorn he regaled,
   On pippin's russet peel,
And, when his juicy salads failed,
   Sliced carrot pleased him well.

A Turkey carpet was his lawn,
   Whereon he loved to bound,
To skip and gambol like a fawn,
   And swing his rump around.

His frisking was at evening hours,
   For then he lost his fear,
But most before approaching showers,
   Or when a storm drew near.

Eight years and five round-rolling moons
   He thus saw steal away,
Dozing out all his idle noons,
   And every night at play.

I kept him for his humour's sake,
   For he would oft beguile
My heart of thoughts that made it ache,
   And force me to a smile.

But now beneath his walnut shade
   He finds his long last home,
And waits, in snug concealment laid,
   Till gentler Puss shall come.

He, still more agèd, feels the shocks
    From which no care can save,
And, partner once of Tiney's box,
    Must soon partake his grave.

The Winter Evening

HARK ! 'tis the twanging horn ! O'er yonder bridge,
That with its wearisome but needful length
Bestrides the wintry flood, in which the moon
Sees her unwrinkled face reflected bright,
He comes, the herald of a noisy world,
With spattered boots, strapped waist, and frozen
    locks,
News from all nations lumbering at his back.
True to his charge, the close-packed load behind,
Yet careless what he brings, his one concern
Is to conduct it to the destined inn,
And having dropped the expected bag—pass on.
He whistles as he goes, light-hearted wretch,
Cold and yet cheerful : messenger of grief
Perhaps to thousands, and of joy to some,
To him indifferent whether grief or joy.
Houses in ashes, and the fall of stocks,
Births, deaths, and marriages, epistles wet
With tears that trickled down the writer's cheeks
Fast as the periods from his fluent quill,
Or charged with amorous sighs of absent swains,
Or nymphs responsive, equally affect
His horse and him, unconscious of them all.

But oh the important budget! ushered in
With such heart-shaking music, who can say
What are its tidings? have our troops awaked?
Or do they still, as if with opium drugged,
Snore to the murmurs of the Atlantic wave?
Is India free? and does she wear her plumed
And jewelled turban with a smile of peace,
Or do we grind her still? The grand debate,
The popular harangue, the tart reply,
The logic, and the wisdom, and the wit,
And the loud laugh—I long to know them all;
I burn to set the imprisoned wranglers free,
And give them voice and utterance once again.

Now stir the fire, and close the shutters fast,
Let fall the curtains, wheel the sofa round,
And while the bubbling and loud hissing urn
Throws up a steamy column, and the cups
That cheer but not inebriate, wait on each,
So let us welcome peaceful evening in.

THE TASK.

The Dog and the Water-Lily

No Fable

THE noon was shady, and soft airs
    Swept Ouse's silent tide,
When, 'scaped from literary cares,
    I wandered on his side.

WILLIAM COWPER

My spaniel, prettiest of his race,
  And high in pedigree,
(Two nymphs adorned with every grace
  That spaniel found for me).

Now wantoned, lost in flags and reeds,
  Now starting into sight,
Pursued the swallow o'er the meads
  With scarce a slower flight.

It was the time when Ouse displayed
  His lilies newly blown ;
Their beauties I intent surveyed
  And one I wished my own.

With cane extended far, I sought
  To steer it close to land ;
But still the prize, though nearly caught,
  Escaped my eager hand.

Beau marked my unsuccessful pains
  With fixed considerate face,
And puzzling set his puppy brains
  To comprehend the case.

But with a cherup clear and strong
  Dispersing all his dream,
I thence withdrew, and followed long
  The windings of the stream.

My ramble ended, I returned ;
  Beau, trotting far before,
The floating wreath again discerned,
  And plunging left the shore.

I saw him with that lily cropped
  Impatient swim to meet
My quick approach, and soon he dropped
  The treasure at my feet.

Charmed with the sight, " The world," I cried,
  " Shall hear of this thy deed :
My dog shall mortify the pride
  Of man's superior breed :

But chief myself I will enjoin,
  Awake at duty's call,
To show a love as prompt as thine
  To Him who gives me all."

On a Spaniel, called " Beau,"
Killing a Young Bird

A SPANIEL, Beau, that fares like you,
  Well fed, and at his ease,
Should wiser be than to pursue
  Each trifle that he sees.

But you have killed a tiny bird
  Which flew not till to-day,
Against my orders, whom you heard
  Forbidding you the prey.

Nor did you kill that you might eat
  And ease a doggish pain ;

For him, though chased with furious heat,
   You left where he was slain.

Nor was he of the thievish sort,
   Or one whom blood allures,
But innocent was all his sport
   Whom you have torn for yours.

My dog ! what remedy remains,
   Since, teach you all I can,
I see you, after all my pains,
   So much resemble man ?

Beau's Reply

Sir, when I flew to seize the bird
   In spite of your command,
A louder voice than yours I heard,
   And harder to withstand.

You cried " Forbear ! "—but in my breast
   A mightier cried " Proceed ! "—
'Twas Nature, sir, whose strong behest
   Impelled me to the deed.

Yet much as Nature I respect,
   I ventured once to break
(As you perhaps may recollect)
   Her precept for your sake ;

179

And when your linnet on a day,
  Passing his prison door,
Had fluttered all his strength away,
  And panting pressed the floor,

Well knowing him a sacred thing,
  Not destined to my tooth,
I only kissed his ruffled wing,
  And licked the feathers smooth.

Let my obedience then excuse
  My disobedience now,
Nor some reproof yourself refuse
  From your aggrieved Bow-wow ;

If killing birds be such a crime
  (Which I can hardly see),
What think you, sir, of killing Time
  With verse addressed to me ?

The Retired Cat

A POET's cat, sedate and grave
As poet well could wish to have,
Was much addicted to inquire
For nooks to which she might retire,
And where, secure as mouse in chink,
She might repose, and sit and think.
I know not where she caught the trick—
Nature perhaps herself had cast her

In such a mould PHILOSOPHIQUE,
Or else she learned it from her master.
Sometimes ascending, debonair,
An apple-tree or lofty pear,
Lodged with convenience in the fork,
She watched the gardener at his work ;
Sometimes her ease and solace sought
In an old empty watering-pot ;
There, wanting nothing save a fan
To seem some nymph in her sedan,
Apparelled in exactest sort,
And ready to be borne to court.

But love of change, it seems, has place
Not only in our wiser race ;
Cats also feel, as well as we,
That passion's force, and so did she.
Her climbing, she began to find,
Exposed her too much to the wind,
And the old utensil of tin
Was cold and comfortless within :
She therefore wished instead of those
Some place of more serene repose,
Where neither cold might come, nor air
Too rudely wanton with her hair,
And sought it in the likeliest mode
Within her master's snug abode.

A drawer, it chanced, at bottom lined
With linen of the softest kind,
With such as merchants introduce
From India, for the ladies' use—
A drawer impending o'er the rest,
Half open in the topmost chest,

Of depth enough, and none to spare,
Invited her to slumber there ;
Puss with delight beyond expression
Surveyed the scene, and took possession.
Recumbent at her ease ere long,
And lulled by her own humdrum song,
She left the cares of life behind,
And slept as she would sleep her last,
When in came, housewifely inclined,
The chambermaid, and shut it fast,
By no malignity impelled,
But all unconscious whom it held.

   Awakened by the shock, cried Puss,
" Was ever cat attended thus !
" The open drawer was left, I see,
" Merely to prove a nest for me.
" For soon as I was well composed
" Then came the maid, and it was closed.
" How smooth these 'kerchiefs, and how sweet !
" Oh, what a delicate retreat !
" I will resign myself to rest
" Till Sol, declining in the west,
" Shall call to supper, when, no doubt,
" Susan will come and let me out."

   The evening came, the sun descended,
And puss remained still unattended.
The night rolled tardily away,
(With her indeed 'twas never day,)
The sprightly morn her course renewed,
The evening gray again ensued,
And puss came into mind no more
Than if entombed the day before.

With hunger pinched, and pinched for room,
She now presaged approaching doom,
Nor slept a single wink, or purred,
Conscious of jeopardy incurred.
   That night, by chance, the poet watching,
Heard an inexplicable scratching ;
His noble heart went pit-a-pat,
And to himself he said—" What's that ? "
He drew the curtain at his side,
And forth he peeped, but nothing spied ;
Yet, by his ear directed, guessed
Something imprisoned in the chest,
And, doubtful what, with prudent care
Resolved it should continue there.
At length, a voice which well he knew,
A long and melancholy mew,
Saluting his poetic ears,
Consoled him, and dispelled his fears ;
He left his bed, he trod the floor,
He 'gan in haste the drawers explore,
The lowest first, and without stop
For 'tis a truth well known to most,
That whatsoever thing is lost,
We seek it, ere it come to light,
In every cranny but the right.
Forth skipped the cat, not now replete
As erst with airy self-conceit,
Nor in her own fond apprehension
A theme for all the world's attention,
But modest, sober, cured of all
Her notions hyperbolical,
And wishing for a place of rest

Anything rather than a chest.
Then stepped the poet into bed,
With this reflection in his head :

Moral

Beware of too sublime a sense
Of your own worth and consequence.
The man who dreams himself so great,
And his importance of such weight,
That all around in all that's done
Must move and act for him alone,
Will learn in school of tribulation
The folly of his expectation.

On a Battered Beauty

HAIR, wax, rouge, honey, teeth you buy,
    A multifarious store !
A mask at once would all supply,
    Nor would it cost you more.

John Gilpin

JOHN GILPIN was a citizen
    Of credit and renown,
A train-band captain eke was he
    Of famous London town.

WILLIAM COWPER

John Gilpin's spouse said to her dear,
  "Though wedded we have been
These twice ten tedious years, yet we
  No holiday have seen.

"To-morrow is our wedding-day,
  And we will then repair
Unto the Bell at Edmonton,
  All in a chaise and pair.

"My sister, and my sister's child,
  Myself, and children three,
Will fill the chaise ; so you must ride
  On horseback after we."

He soon replied, "I do admire
  Of womankind, but one,
And you are she, my dearest dear,
  Therefore it shall be done.

"I am a linen-draper bold,
  As all the world doth know,
And my good friend the calender
  Will lend his horse to go."

Quoth Mrs. Gilpin, "That's well said ;
  And for that wine is dear,
We will be furnished with our own,
  Which is both bright and clear."

John Gilpin kissed his loving wife ;
  O'erjoyed was he to find,
That though on pleasure she was bent,
  She had a frugal mind.

The morning came, the chaise was brought,
  But yet was not allowed
To drive up to the door, lest all
  Should say that she was proud.

So three doors off the chaise was stayed,
  Where they did all get in ;
Six precious souls, and all agog
  To dash through thick and thin.

Smack went the whip, round went the wheels,
  Were never folk so glad,
The stones did rattle underneath,
  As if Cheapside were mad.

John Gilpin at his horse's side
  Seized fast the flowing mane,
And up he got, in haste to ride,
  But soon came down again ;

For saddle-tree scarce reached had he,
  His journey to begin,
When, turning round his head, he saw
  Three customers come in.

So down he came ; for loss of time,
  Although it grieved him sore,
Yet loss of pence, full well he knew,
  Would trouble him much more.

'Twas long before the customers
  Were suited to their mind,
When Betty screaming came down stairs,
  " The wine is left behind ! "

" Good lack ! " quoth he—" yet bring it me,
  My leathern belt likewise,
In which I bear my trusty sword,
  When I do exercise."

Now Mistress Gilpin (careful soul !)
  Had two stone bottles found,
To hold the liquor that she loved,
  And keep it safe and sound.

Each bottle had a curling ear,
  Through which the belt he drew,
And hung a bottle on each side,
  To make his balance true.

Then over all, that he might be
  Equipped from top to toe,
His long red cloak, well brushed and neat,
  He manfully did throw.

Now see him mounted once again
  Upon his nimble steed,
Full slowly pacing o'er the stones,
  With caution and good heed.

But finding soon a smoother road
  Beneath his well-shod feet,
The snorting beast began to trot,
  Which galled him in his seat.

So, " Fair and softly," John he cried,
  But John he cried in vain ;
That trot became a gallop soon,
  In spite of curb and rein.

WILLIAM COWPER

So stooping down, as needs he must
　Who cannot sit upright.
He grasped the mane with both his hands.
　And eke with all his might.

His horse, who never in that sort
　Had handled been before,
What thing upon his back had got
　Did wonder more and more.

Away went Gilpin, neck or nought ;
　Away went hat and wig ;
He little dreamt, when he set out,
　Of running such a rig.

The wind did blow, the cloak did fly,
　Like streamer long and gay,
Till, loop and button failing both,
　At last it flew away.

Then might all people well discern
　The bottles he had slung ;
A bottle swinging at each side,
　As hath been said or sung.

The dogs did bark, the children screamed,
　Up flew the windows all ;
And every soul cried out, " Well done ! "
　As loud as he could bawl.

Away went Gilpin—who but he ?
　His fame soon spread around ;
" He carries weight ! "　" He rides a race ! "
　" 'Tis for a thousand pound ! "

And still, as fast as he drew near,
  'Twas wonderful to view,
How in a trice the turnpike-men
  Their gates wide open threw.

And now, as he went bowing down
  His reeking head full low,
The bottles twain behind his back
  Were shattered at a blow.

Down ran the wine into the road,
  Most piteous to be seen,
Which made his horse's flanks to smoke
  As they had basted been.

But still he seemed to carry weight,
  With leathern girdle braced ;
For all might see the bottle-necks
  Still dangling at his waist.

Thus all through merry Islington
  These gambols he did play,
Until he came unto the Wash
  Of Edmonton so gay ;

And there he threw the Wash about
  On both sides of the way,
Just like unto a trundling mop,
  Or a wild goose at play.

At Edmonton his loving wife
  From the balcony spied
Her tender husband, wondering much
  To see how he did ride.

'Stop, stop, John Gilpin!—Here's the house! "
  They all at once did cry;
" The dinner waits, and we are tired."—
  Said Gilpin—" So am I ! "

But yet his horse was not a whit
  Inclined to tarry there !
For why?—his owner had a house
  Full ten miles off, at Ware.

So like an arrow swift he flew,
  Shot by an archer strong ;
So did he fly—which brings me to
  The middle of my song.

Away went Gilpin, out of breath,
  And sore against his will,
Till at his friend the calender's
  His horse at last stood still.

The calender, amazed to see
  His neighbour in such trim,
Laid down his pipe, flew to the gate,
  And thus accosted him :

" What news ? what news ? your tidings tell ;
  Tell me you must and shall—
Say why bareheaded you are come,
  Or why you come at all ? "

Now Gilpin had a pleasant wit,
  And loved a timely joke ;
And thus unto the calender
  In merry guise he spoke :

"I came because your horse would come,
  And, if I well forebode,
My hat and wig will soon be here,—
  They are upon the road."

The calender, right glad to find
  His friend in merry pin,
Returned him not a single word,
  But to the house went in ;

Whence straight he came with hat and wig ;
  A wig that flowed behind,
A hat not much the worse for wear,
  Each comely in its kind.

He held them up, and in his turn
  Thus showed his ready wit,
"My head is twice as big as yours,
  They therefore needs must fit.

"But let me scrape the dirt away
  That hangs upon your face ;
And stop and eat, for well you may
  Be in a hungry case."

Said John, "It is my wedding-day,
  And all the world would stare,
If wife should dine at Edmonton,
  And I should dine at Ware."

So turning to his horse, he said,
  "I am in haste to dine ;
'Twas for your pleasure you came here,
  You shall go back for mine."

Ah, luckless speech, and bootless boast !
  For which he paid full dear ;
For, while he spake, a braying ass
  Did sing most loud and clear ;

Whereat his horse did snort, as he
  Had heard a lion roar,
And galloped off with all his might,
  As he had done before.

Away went Gilpin, and away
  Went Gilpin's hat and wig ;
He lost them sooner than at first ;
  For why ?—they were too big.

Now Mistress Gilpin, when she saw
  Her husband posting down
Into the country far away,
  She pulled out half a crown ;

And thus unto the youth she said
  That drove them to the Bell,
" This shall be yours, when you bring back
  My husband safe and well."

The youth did ride, and soon did meet
  John coming back amain :
Whom in a trice he tried to stop,
  By catching at his rein ;

But not performing what he meant,
  And gladly would have done,
The frighted steed he frighted more,
  And made him faster run.

Away went Gilpin, and away
  Went postboy at his heels,
The postboy's horse right glad to miss
  The lumbering of the wheels.

Six gentlemen upon the road,
  Thus seeing Gilpin fly,
With postboy scampering in the rear,
  They raised the hue and cry :

" Stop thief ! stop thief !—a highwayman ! "
  Not one of them was mute ;
And all and each that passed that way
  Did join in the pursuit.

And now the turnpike gates again
  Flew open in short space ;
The toll-men thinking, as before,
  That Gilpin rode a race.

And so he did, and won it too,
  For he got first to town ;
Nor stopped till where he had got up
  He did again get down.

Now let us sing, Long live the king !
  And Gilpin, long live he !
And when he next doth ride abroad
  May I be there to see.

WILLIAM COWPER

The Good Companion

From *Friendship*

THE man that hails you Tom or Jack,
And proves by thumps upon your back
   How he esteems your merit,
Is such a friend that one had need
Be very much his friend indeed,
   To pardon or to bear it.

ERASMUS DARWIN

1731–1802

Steam Power

SOON shall thy arm, UNCONQUER'D STEAM ! afar
Drag the slow barge, or drive the rapid car ;
Or on wide-waving wings expanded bear
The flying-chariot through the fields of air.
—Fair crews triumphant, leaning from above,
Shall wave their fluttering kerchiefs as they move ;
Or warrior-bands alarm the gaping crowd,
And armies shrink beneath the shadowy cloud.

THE ECONOMY OF VEGETATION, I.

ERASMUS DARWIN

Flowers of the Sky

ROLL on, YE STARS ! exult in youthful prime,
Mark with bright curves the printless steps of Time ;
Near and more near your beamy cars approach,
And lessening orbs on lessening orbs encroach ;—
Flowers of the sky ! ye too to age must yield,
Frail as your silken sisters of the field !
Star after star from Heaven's high arch shall rush,
Suns sink on suns, and systems systems crush,
Headlong, extinct, to one dark centre fall,
And Death and Night and Chaos mingle all !
—Till o'er the wreck, emerging from the storm,
Immortal NATURE lifts her changeful form,
Mounts from her funeral pyre on wings of flame,
And soars and shines, another and the same.

THE ECONOMY OF VEGETATION, IV.

RICHARD BRINSLEY SHERIDAN

1751–1816

Song

HERE's to the maiden of bashful fifteen ;
   Here's to the widow of fifty ;
Here's to the flaunting extravagant quean,
   And here's to the housewife that's thrifty.

Chorus.

   Let the toast pass,—
   Drink to the lass,
I'll warrant she'll prove an excuse for the glass.

RICHARD BRINSLEY SHERIDAN

Here's to the charmer whose dimples we prize ;
   Now to the maid who has none, sir :
Here's to the girl with a pair of blue eyes,
   And here's to the nymph with but *one*, sir.
    Chorus. Let the toast pass, &c.

Here's to the maid with a bosom of snow ;
   Now to her that's as brown as a berry :
Here's to the wife with a face full of woe,
   And now to the girl that is merry.
    Chorus. Let the toast pass, &c.

For let 'em be clumsy, or let 'em be slim,
   Young or ancient, I care not a feather ;
So fill a pint bumper quite up to the brim,
   And let us e'en toast them together.
    Chorus. Let the toast pass, &c.

           THE SCHOOL FOR SCANDAL, ACT III.

THOMAS CHATTERTON
1752–1770

To Horace Walpole

WALPOLE, I thought not I should ever see
So mean a heart as thine has proved to be.
Thou who, in luxury nursed, behold'st with scorn
The boy, who, friendless, fatherless, forlorn,
Asks thy high favour—thou mayest call me cheat.
Say, didst thou never practise such deceit ?

THOMAS CHATTERTON

Who wrote Otranto? but I will not chide:
Scorn I'll repay with scorn, and pride with pride.
Still, Walpole, still thy prosy chapters write,
And twaddling letters to some fair indite;
Laud all above thee, fawn and cringe to those
Who, for thy fame, were better friends than foes;
Still spurn th' incautious fool who dares—

*　　*　　*

Had I the gifts of wealth and luxury shared,
Not poor and mean, Walpole! thou hadst not dared
Thus to insult. But I shall live and stand
By Rowley's side, when thou art dead and damned.

From *To a Friend on his Intended Marriage*

MARRIAGE, dear Mason, is a serious thing;
　'Tis proper every man should think it so;
'Twill either every human blessing bring,
　Or load thee with a settlement of woe.

Sometimes indeed it is a middle state,
　Neither supremely blest, nor deeply cursed;
A stagnant pool of life, a dream of fate:
　In my opinion, of all states the worst.

THOMAS CHATTERTON

The Copernican System

THE sun revolving on his axis turns,
And with creative fire intensely burns ;
Impelled the forcive air, our breath supreme
Rolls with the planets round the solar gleam.
First Mercury completes his transient year,
Glowing, refulgent, with reflected glare ;
Bright Venus occupies a wider way,
The early harbinger of night and day ;
More distant still, our globe terraqueous turns,
Nor chills intense, nor fiercely heated burns ;
Around her rolls the lunar orb of light,
Trailing her silver glories through the night.
On the earth's orbit see the various signs,
Mark where the sun, our year completing, shines ;
First the bright Ram his languid ray improves ;
Next glaring watery, through the Bull he moves ;
The amorous Twins admit his genial ray ;
Now burning, through the Crab he takes his way ;
The Lion flaming, bears the solar power ;
The Virgin faints beneath the sultry shower.
Now the just Balance weighs his equal force,
The slimy Serpent swelters in his course ;
The sabled Archer clouds his languid face ;
The Goat, with tempests, urges on his race ;
Now in the Waterer his faint beams appear,
And the cold Fishes end the circling year.
Beyond our globe, the sanguine Mars displays
A strong reflection of primaeval rays ;
Next belted Jupiter far distant gleams,

Scarcely enlightened with the solar beams ;
With four unfixed receptacles of light,
He tours majestic through the spacious height ;
But farther yet the tardy Saturn lags,
And five attendant luminaries drags ;
Investing with a double ring his pace,
He circles through immensity of space.

These are Thy wondrous works, first Source of God.
Now more admired in being understood.

Last Verses

FAREWELL, Bristolia's dingy piles of brick,
Lovers of mammon, worshippers of trick !
Ye spurned the boy who gave you antique lays,
And paid for learning with your empty praise.
Farewell, ye guzzling aldermanic fools,
By nature fitted for corruption's tools !
I go to where celestial anthems swell ;
But you, when you depart, will sink to hell.
Farewell, my mother !—cease, my anguished soul,
Nor let distraction's billows o'er me roll !
Have mercy, Heaven ! when here I cease to live,
And this last act of wretchedness forgive.

THOMAS RUSSELL

1762-1788

Lament from The Maniac

WHEN thirst and hunger griev'd her most,
  If any food she took,
It was the berry from the thorn,
  The water from the brook.

Now hurrying o'er the heath she hied,
  Now wander'd thro' the wood,
Now o'er the precipice she peep'd,
  Now stood and eyed the flood.

From every hedge a flower she pluck'd,
  And moss from every stone,
To make a garland for her Love,
  Yet left it still undone.

Still, as she rambled, was she wont
  To trill a plaintive song,
'Twas wild, and full of fancies vain,
  Yet suited well her wrong.

All loose, yet lovely, to the wind
  Her golden tresses flew,
And now alas ! with heat were scorch'd,
  And now were drench'd with dew.

No Friend was left the tears to wipe
  That dimm'd her radiant eyes,
Yet oft their beams like those would shine
  That gleam from watry skies.

THOMAS RUSSELL

Oft too a smile, but not of joy,
  Play'd on her brow o'ercast ;
It was the faint cold smile of Spring,
  Ere Winter yet is past.

Those sorrows, which her tongue conceal'd,
  Her broken sighs confest ;
Her cloak was too much torn to hide
  The throbbings of her breast.

From all, who near her chanc'd to stray,
  With wild affright she ran ;
Each voice that reach'd her scar'd her breast,
  But most the voice of Man.

To me alone, when oft we met,
  Her ear she would incline,
And with me weep, for well she knew
  Her woes resembled mine.

One morn I sought her ; but too late—
  Her wound had bled so sore—
God rest thy Spirit, gentle Maid !
  Thou'rt gone for evermore !

SONNETS AND MISCELLANEOUS POEMS.

WILLIAM BLAKE

1757–1827

Song

My silks and fine array,
My smiles and languish'd air,
By love are driv'n away;
And mournful lean Despair
Brings me yew to deck my grave:
Such end true lovers have.

His face is fair as heav'n
When springing buds unfold;
O why to him was't giv'n
Whose heart is wintry cold?
His breast is love's all worship'd tomb,
Where all love's pilgrims come.

Bring me an axe and spade,
Bring me a winding sheet;
When I my grave have made
Let winds and tempests beat:
Then down I'll lie as cold as clay.
True love doth pass away!

POETICAL SKETCHES.

To the Muses

WHETHER on Ida's shady brow,
Or in the chambers of the East,
The chambers of the sun, that now
From antient melody have ceas'd;

Whether in Heav'n ye wander fair,
Or the green corners of the earth,
Or the blue regions of the air
Where the melodious winds have birth ;

Whether on chrystal rocks ye rove,
Beneath the bosom of the sea
Wand'ring in many a coral grove,
Fair Nine, forsaking Poetry !

How have you left the antient love
That bards of old enjoy'd in you !
The languid strings do scarcely move !
The sound is forc'd, the notes are few !

POETICAL SKETCHES.

Piping down the Valleys wild

PIPING down the valleys wild,
Piping songs of pleasant glee,
On a cloud I saw a child,
And he laughing said to me :

' Pipe a song about a Lamb ! '
So I piped with merry chear.
' Piper, pipe that song again ' ;
So I piped : he wept to hear.

' Drop thy pipe, thy happy pipe ;
Sing thy songs of happy chear ' :
So I sang the same again,
While he wept with joy to hear.

' Piper, sit thee down and write
In a book, that all may read.'
So he vanish'd from my sight,
And I pluck'd a hollow reed,

And I made a rural pen,
And I stain'd the water clear,
And I wrote my happy songs
Every child may joy to hear.

SONGS OF INNOCENCE.

The Little Black Boy

My mother bore me in the southern wild,
And I am black, but O my soul is white
White as an angel is the English child,
But I am black, as if bereav'd of light.

My mother taught me underneath a tree,
And, sitting down before the heat of day,
She took me on her lap and kissèd me,
And, pointing to the east, began to say :

' Look on the rising sun,—there God does live,
And gives his light, and gives his heat away ;
And flowers and trees and beasts and men receive
Comfort in morning, joy in the noon day.

' And we are put on earth a little space,
That we may learn to bear the beams of love ;
And these black bodies and this sun-burnt face
Is but a cloud, and like a shady grove.

' For when our souls have learn'd the heat to bear,
The cloud will vanish, we shall hear his voice,
Saying : " come out from the grove, my love and care,
And round my golden tent like lambs rejoice." '

Thus did my mother say, and kissèd me ;
And thus I say to little English boy.
When I from black, and he from white cloud free,
And round the tent of God like lambs we joy,

I'll shade him from the heat, till he can bear
To lean in joy upon our father's knee ;
And then I'll stand and stroke his silver hair,
And be like him, and he will then love me.

SONGS OF INNOCENCE.

A Dream

ONCE a dream did weave a shade
O'er my Angel-guarded bed,
That an Emmet lost its way
Where on grass methought I lay.

Troubled, 'wilder'd, and forlorn,
Dark, benighted, travel-worn,
Over many a tangled spray,
All heart-broke I heard her say :

" O, my children ! do they cry ?
" Do they hear their father sigh ?
" Now they look abroad to see :
" Now return and weep for me."

Pitying, I drop'd a tear ;
But I saw a glow-worm near,
Who replied : " What wailing wight
" Calls the watchman of the night ?

" I am set to light the ground,
" While the beetle goes his round :
" Follow now the beetle's hum ;
" Little wanderer, hie thee home."

SONGS OF INNOCENCE.

The Little Girl Lost

In futurity
I prophetic see
That the earth from sleep
(Grave the sentence deep)

Shall arise and seek
For her maker meek ;
And the desart wild
Become a garden mild.

In the southern clime,
Where the summer's prime
Never fades away,
Lovely Lyca lay.

Seven summers old
Lovely Lyca told ;
She had wander'd long
Hearing wild birds' song.

" Sweet sleep, come to me
" Underneath this tree.
" Do father, mother, weep?
" Where can Lyca sleep?

" Lost in desart wild
" Is your little child.
" How can Lyca sleep
" If her mother weep?

" If her heart does ake
" Then let Lyca wake;
" If my mother sleep,
" Lyca shall not weep.

" Frowning, frowning night,
" O'er this desart bright
" Let thy moon arise
" While I close my eyes."

Sleeping Lyca lay
While the beasts of prey,
Come from caverns deep,
View'd the maid asleep.

The kingly lion stood
And the virgin view'd,
Then he gamboll'd round
O'er the hallow'd ground.

Leopards, tygers, play
Round her as she lay,
While the lion old
Bow'd his mane of gold

And her bosom lick,
And upon her neck
From his eyes of flame
Ruby tears there came ;

While the lioness
Loos'd her slender dress,
And naked they convey'd
To caves the sleeping maid.

SONGS OF INNOCENCE.

Holy Thursday

'Twas on a Holy Thursday, their innocent faces clean,
The children walking two & two, in red & blue &
    green,
Grey headed beadles walk'd before, with wands as
    white as snow,
Till into the high dome of Paul's they like Thames'
    waters flow.

O what a multitude they seem'd, these flowers of
    London town !
Seated in companies, they sit with radiance all their
    own.
The hum of multitudes was there, but multitudes of
    lambs,
Thousands of little boys & girls raising their
    innocent hands.

Now like a mighty wind they raise to heaven the voice
    of song,
Or like harmonious thunderings the seats of heaven
    among.
Beneath them sit the agèd men, wise guardians of the
    poor ;
Then cherish pity, lest you drive an angel from your
    door.

SONGS OF INNOCENCE.

Night

THE sun descending in the west,
The evening star does shine ;
The birds are silent in their nest,
And I must seek for mine.
The moon, like a flower,
In heaven's high bower,
With silent delight
Sits and smiles on the night.

Farewell, green fields and happy groves,
Where flocks have took delight.
Where lambs have nibbled, silent moves
The feet of angels bright ;
Unseen they pour blessing,
And joy without ceasing,
On each bud and blossom,
And each sleeping bosom.

They look in every thoughtless nest,
Where birds are cover'd warm ;
They visit caves of every beast,
To keep them all from harm.
If they see any weeping
That should have been sleeping,
They pour sleep on their head,
And sit down by their bed.

When wolves and tygers howl for prey,
They pitying stand and weep ;
Seeking to drive their thirst away,
And keep them from the sheep
But if they rush dreadful,
The angels, most heedful,
Receive each mild spirit,
New worlds to inherit.

And there the lion's ruddy eyes
Shall flow with tears of gold,
And pitying the tender cries,
And walking round the fold,
Saying ' wrath, by his meekness,
And, by his health, sickness
Is driven away
From our immortal day.

' And now beside thee, bleating lamb,
I can lie down and sleep ;
Or think on him who bore thy name,
Graze after thee and weep.

For, wash'd in life's river,
My bright mane for ever
Shall shine like the gold
As I guard o'er the fold.'

SONGS OF INNOCENCE.

Hear the Voice of the Bard

HEAR the voice of the Bard !
Who Present, Past, and Future, sees ;
Whose ears have heard
The Holy Word
That walk'd among the ancient trees,

Calling the lapsèd Soul,
And weeping in the evening dew ;
That might controll
The starry pole,
And fallen fallen light renew !

' O Earth, O Earth, return !
Arise from out the dewy grass ;
Night is worn,
And the morn
Rises from the slumberous mass.

' Turn away no more ;
Why wilt thou turn away ?
The starry floor,
The wat'ry shore,
Is giv'n thee till the break of day.'

SONGS OF EXPERIENCE.

WILLIAM BLAKE

The Sick Rose

O ROSE, thou art sick;
The invisible worm,
That flies in the night,
In the howling storm,

Hath found out thy bed
Of crimson joy;
And her dark secret love
Does thy life destroy.

SONGS OF EXPERIENCE.

The Tiger

TYGER! Tyger! burning bright
In the forests of the night,
What immortal hand or eye
Could frame thy fearful symmetry?

In what distant deeps or skies
Burnt the fire of thine eyes?
On what wings dare he aspire?
What the hand dare seize the fire,

And what shoulder, and what art,
Could twist the sinews of thy heart?
And when thy heart began to beat,
What dread hand? and what dread feet?

What the hammer? what the chain?
In what furnace was thy brain?
What the anvil? what dread grasp
Dare its deadly terrors clasp?

When the stars threw down their spears,
And water'd heaven with their tears,
Did he smile his work to see?
Did he who made the Lamb make thee?

Tyger! Tyger! burning bright
In the forests of the night,
What immortal hand or eye,
Dare frame thy fearful symmetry?

SONGS OF EXPERIENCE.

The Clod and the Pebble

' Love seeketh not Itself to please,
Nor for itself hath any care,
But for another gives its ease,
And builds a Heaven in Hell's despair.'

So sung a little Clod of Clay,
Trodden with the cattle's feet,
But a Peeble of the brook
Warbled out these metres meet:

' Love seeketh only Self to please,
To bind another to Its delight,
Joys in another's loss of ease,
And builds a Hell in Heaven's despite.'

SONGS OF EXPERIENCE.

WILLIAM BLAKE

Ah! Sun-Flower

Ah, Sun-flower! weary of time,
Who countest the steps of the Sun;
Seeking after that sweet golden clime,
Where the traveller's journey is done;

Where the Youth pined away with desire,
And the pale Virgin shrouded in snow,
Arise from their graves, and aspire
Where my Sun-flower wishes to go.

SONGS OF EXPERIENCE.

Never Seek to Tell thy Love

Never seek to tell thy love,
Love that never told can be;
For the gentle wind does move
Silently, invisibly.

I told my love, I told my love,
I told her all my heart;
Trembling, cold, in ghastly fears,
Ah! she doth depart.

Soon as she was gone from me,
A traveller came by,
Silently, invisibly:
He took her with a sigh.

WILLIAM BLAKE

Several Questions Answer'd

He who bends to himself a joy
Doth the winged life destroy ;
But he who kisses the joy as it flies
Lives in Eternity's sun rise.

The look of love alarms
Because 'tis fill'd with fire ;
But the look of soft deceit
Shall Win the lover's hire.

Soft deceit and Idleness,
These are Beauty's sweetest dress.

What is it men in women do require ?
The lineaments of Gratified Desire.
What is it women do in men require ?
The lineaments of Gratified Desire.

Remove away that black'ning church,
Remove away that marriage hearse
Remove away that * * * * of blood,
You'll quite remove the ancient curse.

FROM THE ROSETTI MS.

WILLIAM BLAKE

The Thoughts of Man

" WITH what sense is it that the chicken shuns the
    ravenous hawk ?
" With what sense does the tame pigeon measure out
    the expanse ?
" With what sense does the bee form cells ? have not
    the mouse & frog
" Eyes and ears and sense of touch ? yet are their
    habitations
" And their pursuits as different as their forms and
    as their joys.
" Ask the wild ass why he refuses burdens, and the
    meek camel
" Why he loves man : is it because of eye, ear,
    mouth, or skin,
" Or breathing nostrils ? No, for these the wolf and
    tyger have.
" Ask the blind worm the secrets of the grave, and
    why her spires
" Love to curl round the bones of death ; and ask
    the rav'nous snake
" Where she gets poison, & the wing'd eagle why
    he loves the sun ;
" And then tell me the thoughts of man, that have
    been hid of old."

VISIONS OF THE DAUGHTERS OF ALBION.

WILLIAM BLAKE

London

I WANDER thro' each charter'd street,
Near where the charter'd Thames does flow,
And mark in every face I meet
Marks of weakness, marks of woe.

In every cry of every Man,
In every Infant's cry of fear,
In every voice, in every ban,
The mind-forg'd manacles I hear.

How the Chimney-sweeper's cry
Every black'ning Church appalls ;
And the hapless Soldier's sigh
Runs in blood down Palace walls.

But most thro' midnight streets I hear
How the youthful Harlot's curse
Blasts the new born Infant's tear,
And blights with plagues the Marriage hearse.

SONGS OF EXPERIENCE.

Infant Sorrow

My mother groan'd ! my father wept.
Into the dangerous world I leapt :
Helpless, naked, piping loud :
Like a fiend hid in a cloud.

Struggling in my father's hands,
Striving against my swadling bands,
Bound and weary I thought best
To sulk upon my mother's breast.

When I saw that rage was vain,
And to sulk would nothing gain,
Turning many a trick and wile,
I began to soothe and smile.

And I sooth'd day after day
Till upon the ground I stray;
And I smil'd night after night,
Seeking only for delight.

And I saw before me shine
Clusters of the wand'ring vine
And many a lovely flower and tree
Stretch'd their blossoms out to me.

My father then with holy look,
In his hands a holy book,
Pronounc'd curses on my head
And bound me in a mirtle shade.

I beheld the Priests by night;
They embrac'd the blossoms bright:
I beheld the Priests by day
Underneath the vines they lay.

So I smote them and their gore
Stain'd the roots my mirtle bore;
But the time of youth is fled,
And grey hairs are on my head.

SONGS OF EXPERIENCE.

WILLIAM BLAKE

To my Mirtle

To a lovely mirtle bound,
Blossoms show'ring all around,
O, How sick and weary I
Underneath my mirtle lie.
Why should I be bound to thee,
O, my lovely mirtle tree?

A Poison Tree

I was angry with my friend :
I told my wrath, my wrath did end.
I was angry with my foe :
I told it not, my wrath did grow.

And I water'd it in fears,
Night and morning with my tears ;
And I sunnèd it with smiles,
And with soft deceitful wiles.

And it grew both day and night,
Till it bore an apple bright ;
And my foe beheld it shine,
And he knew that it was mine,

And into my garden stole
When the night had veil'd the pole :
In the morning glad I see
My foe outstretch'd beneath the tree.

SONGS OF EXPERIENCE.

ROBERT BURNS

1759–1796

Green grow the Rashes O

GREEN grow the rashes O,
   Green grow the rashes O ;
The sweetest hours that e'er I spend,
   Are spent amang the lasses O !

There's nought but care on ev'ry han',
   In ev'ry hour that passes O ;
What signifies the life o' man,
   An' 'twere na for the lasses O.

The warly race may riches chase,
   An' riches still may fly them O ;
An' tho' at last they catch them fast,
   Their hearts can ne'er enjoy them O.

But gie me a canny hour at e'en,
   My arms about my dearie O ;
An' warly cares, an' warly men,
   May a' gae tapsalteerie O !

For you sae douce, ye sneer at this,
   Ye're nought but senseless asses O :
The wisest man the warl' saw,
   He dearly lov'd the lasses O.

Auld nature swears, the lovely dears
   Her noblest work she classes O ;
Her prentice han' she tried on man,
   An' then she made the lasses O.

warly] worldly   tapsalteerie] topsy-turvy

ROBERT BURNS

Auld Lang Syne

SHOULD auld acquaintance be forgot,
  And never brought to min' ?
Should auld acquaintance be forgot,
  And days o' lang syne ?

  For auld lang syne, my dear.
    For auld lang syne,
  We'll tak a cup o' kindness yet,
    For auld lang syne.

We twa hae run about the braes,
  And pu'd the gowans fine ;
But we've wander'd mony a weary foot
  Sin' auld lang syne.

We twa hae paidled i' the burn,
  From morning sun till dine ;
But seas between us braid hae roar'd
  Sin' auld lang syne.

And there's a hand, my trusty fiere,
  And gie 's a hand o' thine ;
And we'll tak a right guid-willie waught,
  For auld lang syne.

And surely ye'll be your pint-stowp,
  And surely I'll be mine ;
And we'll tak a cup o' kindness yet
  For auld lang syne.

THE SCOTS MUSICAL MUSEUM, V.

  gowans] daisies   paidled] paddled   dine] dinner   fiere]
companion   guid-willie waught] hearty draught   ye'll be]
you will be good for

ROBERT BURNS

Of a' the Airts

Of a' the airts the wind can blaw,
  I dearly like the west,
For there the bonnie lassie lives,
  The lassie I lo'e best :
There 's wild woods grow, and rivers row,
  And mony a hill between ;
But day and night my fancy's flight
  Is ever wi' my Jean.

I see her in the dewy flowers,
  I see her sweet and fair :
I hear her in the tunefu' birds,
  I hear her charm the air :
There 's not a bonnie flower that springs
  By fountain, shaw, or green ;
There 's not a bonnie bird that sings,
  But minds me o' my Jean.

THE SCOTS MUSICAL MUSEUM, III.

airts] points of the compass   row] roll

Highland Mary

Ye banks and braes and streams around
  The castle o' Montgomery,
Green be your woods, and fair your flowers,
  Your waters never drumlie !

drumlie] turbid

There simmer first unfauld her robes,
  And there the langest tarry ;
For there I took the last fareweel
  O' my sweet Highland Mary.

How sweetly bloom'd the gay green birk,
  How rich the hawthorn's blossom,
As underneath their fragrant shade
  I clasp'd her to my bosom !
The golden hours on angel wings
  Flew o'er me and my dearie ;
For dear to me as light and life
  Was my sweet Highland Mary.

Wi' mony a vow and lock'd embrace
  Our parting was fu' tender ;
And, pledging aft to meet again,
  We tore oursels asunder ;
But oh ! fell Death's untimely frost,
  That nipt my flower sae early !
Now green's the sod, and cauld's the clay,
  That wraps my Highland Mary !

O pale, pale now, those rosy lips,
  I aft have kiss'd sae fondly !
And closed for aye the sparkling glance,
  That dwelt on me sae kindly !
And mould'ring now in silent dust,
  That heart that lo'ed me dearly !
But still within my bosom's core
  Shall live my Highland Mary.

SELECT COLLECTION OF ORIGINAL SCOTTISH AIRS, II.

ROBERT BURNS
The Banks o' Doon

Ye banks and braes o' bonnie Doon,
　How can ye bloom sae fresh and fair?
How can ye chant, ye little birds,
　And I sae weary fu' o' care?
Thou'lt break my heart, thou warbling bird,
　That wantons thro' the flowering thorn :
Thou minds me o' departed joys,
　Departed never to return.

Aft hae I rov'd by bonnie Doon,
　To see the rose and woodbine twine ;
And ilka bird sang o' its love,
　And fondly sae did I o' mine.
Wi' lightsome heart I pu'd a rose,
　Fu' sweet upon its thorny tree ;
And my fause lover stole my rose,
　But ah ! he left the thorn wi' me.

THE SCOTS MUSICAL MUSEUM, IV.

Ye Flowery Banks

Ye flowery banks o' bonie Doon,
　How can ye blume sae fair?
How can ye chant, ye little birds,
　And I sae fu' o' care?

Thou'll break my heart, thou bonie bird,
　That sings upon the bough :
Thou minds me o' the happy days
　When my fause Luve was true.

224

Thou'll break my heart, thou bonie bird,
  That sings beside thy mate :
For sae I sat, and sae I sang,
  And wist na o' my fate.

Aft hae I rov'd by bonie Doon
  To see the woodbine twine,
And ilka bird sang o' its luve,
  And sae did I o' mine.

Wi' lightsome heart I pu'd a rose
  Frae aff its thorny tree,
And my fause luver staw my rose,
  But left the thorn wi' me.

RELIQUES.

Ae fond Kiss

AE fond kiss, and then we sever !
Ae fareweel, and then for ever !
Deep in heart-wrung tears I'll pledge thee,
Warring sighs and groans I'll wage thee.
Who shall say that Fortune grieves him
While the star of hope she leaves him ?
Me, nae cheerfu' twinkle lights me,
Dark despair around benights me.

I'll ne'er blame my partial fancy,
Naething could resist my Nancy ;
But to see her was to love her,
Love but her, and love for ever.

Had we never lov'd sae kindly,
Had we never lov'd sae blindly,
Never met—or never parted,
We had ne'er been broken-hearted.

Fare thee weel, thou first and fairest !
Fare thee weel, thou best and dearest !
Thine be ilka joy and treasure,
Peace, Enjoyment, Love, and Pleasure.
Ae fond kiss, and then we sever ;
Ae fareweel, alas, for ever !
Deep in heart-wrung tears I'll pledge thee,
Warring sighs and groans I'll wage thee.

THE SCOTS MUSICAL MUSEUM, iv.

A Red, Red Rose

My love is like a red, red rose
  That 's newly sprung in June :
My love is like the melodie
  That 's sweetly play'd in tune.

As fair art thou, my bonnie lass,
  So deep in love am I :
And I will love thee still, my dear,
  Till a' the seas gang dry.

Till a' the seas gang dry, my dear,
  And the rocks melt wi' the sun :
And I will love thee still, my dear,
  While the sands o' life shall run.

And fare thee weel, my only love,
  And fare thee weel a while !
And I will come again, my love,
  Tho' it were ten thousand mile.

THE SCOTS MUSICAL MUSEUM, V.

Bonnie Lesley

O SAW ye bonnie Lesley
  As she gaed o'er the Border ?
She 's gane, like Alexander,
  To spread her conquests farther.

To see her is to love her,
  And love but her for ever ;
For Nature made her what she is,
  And never made anither !

Thou art a queen, fair Lesley,
  Thy subjects we, before thee :
Thou art divine, fair Lesley,
  The hearts o' men adore thee.

The Deil he could na skaith thee,
  Or aught that wad belang thee ;
He'd look into thy bonnie face,
  And say, ' I canna wrang thee.'

The Powers aboon will tent thee ;
  Misfortune sha'na steer thee ;

tent] take care of   steer] molest

227

Thou'rt like themsel' sae lovely,
    That ill they'll ne'er let near thee.

Return again, fair Lesley,
    Return to Caledonie !
That we may brag we hae a lass
    There 's nane again sae bonnie.

SELECT COLLECTION OF ORIGINAL SCOTTISH AIRS.

Epistle to James Smith

DEAR Smith, the sleest, paukie thief,
That e'er attempted stealth or rief,
Ye surely hae some warlock-breef
              Owre human hearts ;
For ne'er a bosom yet was prief
              Against your arts.

For me, I swear by sun an' moon,
And ev'ry star that blinks aboon,
Ye've cost me twenty pair o' shoon
              Just gaun to see you ;
And ev'ry ither pair that's done,
              Mair taen I'm wi' you.

That auld capricious carlin, Nature,
To mak amends for scrimpit stature,

sleest] slyest   paukie] artful   rief] plunder   warlock]
wizard   prief] proof   gaun] going   taen] taken   carlin]
old woman   scrimpit] stinted

She's turn'd you off, a human creature
On her *first* plan,
And in her freaks, on ev'ry feature,
She's wrote, *the Man*.

Just now I've taen the fit o' rhyme,
My barmie noddle's working prime,
My fancy yerkit up sublime
Wi' hasty summon :
Hae ye a leisure-moment's time
To hear what's comin ?

Some rhyme a neebor's name to lash ;
Some rhyme (vain thought !) for needfu' cash ;
Some rhyme to court the countra clash,
An' raise a din ;
For me, an *aim* I never fash ;
I rhyme for fun.

The star that rules my luckless lot,
Has fated me the russet coat,
An' damn'd my fortune to the groat ;
But in requit,
Has blest me wi' a random shot
O' countra wit.

This while my notion's taen a sklent,
To try my fate in guid, black *prent* ;

barmie] fermenting   noddle] head   clash] talk
fash] trouble about   sklent] slant, turn

229

But still the mair I'm that way bent,
          Something cries, ' Hoolie !
' I red you, honest man, tak tent !
             ' Ye'll shaw your folly.

' There 's ither poets, much your betters,
' Far seen in *Greek*, deep men o' letters,
' Hae thought they had ensur'd their debtors,
          ' A' future ages ;
' Now moths deform in shapeless tatters,
          ' Their unknown pages.'

Then farewel hopes o' laurel-boughs,
To garland my poetic brows !
Henceforth I'll rove where busy ploughs
          Are whistling thrang,
An' teach the lanely heights an' howes
          My rustic sang,

I'll wander on with tentless heed
How never-halting moments speed,
Till fate shall snap the brittle thread ;
          Then, all unknown,
I'll lay me with th' inglorious dead,
          Forgot and gone !

But why o' Death begin a tale?
Just now we're living sound and hale ;
Then top and maintop croud the sail,

hoolie] gently   red] advise   tak tent] take care
  thrang] thronged, in plenty   howes] hollows

Heave *Care* o'er-side !
And large, before Enjoyment's gale,
Let's tak the tide.

This life, sae far's I understand,
Is a' enchanted fairy land,
Where Pleasure is the Magic Wand,
That, wielded right,
Maks Hours like Minutes, hand in hand,
Dance by fu' light.

The magic-wand then let us wield ;
For, ance that five-an'-forty's speel'd,
See crazy, weary, joyless Eild,
Wi' wrinkl'd face,
Comes hostin, hirplin owre the field,
Wi' creepin pace.

When ance *life's day* draws near the gloamin,
Then fareweel vacant careless roamin ;
An' fareweel chearfu' tankards foamin,
An' social noise ;
An' fareweel dear, deluding *woman*,
The joy of joys !

O Life ! how pleasant in thy morning,
Young Fancy's rays the hills adorning !
Cold-pausing Caution's lesson scorning,
We frisk away,
Like school-boys, at th' expected warning,
To joy and play.

speel'd] climbed   Eild] Old Age   hostin] coughing
hirplin] creeping   gloamin] twilight

We wander there, we wander here,
We eye the rose upon the brier,
Unmindful that the thorn is near,
   Among the leaves ;
And tho' the puny wound appear,
   Short while it grieves.

Some, lucky, find a flow'ry spot,
For which they never toil'd nor swat ;
They drink the sweet and eat the fat,
   But care or pain ;
And, haply, eye the barren hut
   With high disdain.

With steady aim, some Fortune chase ;
Keen hope does ev'ry sinew brace ;
Thro' fair, thro' foul, they urge the race,
   And seize the prey :
Then canie, in some cozie place,
   They close the *day*.

And others, like your humble servant,
Poor wights ! nae rules nor roads observin ;
To right or left, eternal swervin,
   They zig zag on ;
Till curst with age, obscure an' starvin,
   They aften groan.

Alas ! what bitter toil an' straining—
But truce with peevish, poor complaining !
Is Fortune's fickle *Luna* waning ?

swat] sweated

E'en let her gang !
Beneath what light she has remaining,
Let 's sing our sang.

My pen I here fling to the door,
And kneel, ' Ye Pow'rs ! ' and warm implore,
' Tho' I should wander *Terra* o'er,
' In all her climes,
' Grant me but this, I ask no more,
' Ay rowth o' rhymes.

' Gie dreeping roasts to countra Lairds,
' Till icicles hing frae their beards ;
' Gie fine braw claes to fine Life-guards,
' And Maids of Honor ;
' And yill an' whisky gie to Cairds,
' Until they sconner.

' A Title, *Dempster* merits it ;
' A Garter gie to *Willie Pitt* ;
' Gie wealth to some be-ledger'd Cit,
' In cent. per cent.
' But give me real, sterling Wit,
' And I'm content.

' While Ye are pleas'd to keep me hale,
' I'll sit down o'er my scanty meal,
' Be't *water-brose*, or *muslin-kail*,
' Wi' chearfu' face,
' As lang's the Muses dinna fail
' To say the grace.'

rowth] plenty   claes] clothes   yill] ale   cairds] tinkers
sconner] flinch, feel disgust   muslin-kail] broth made of
water, barley, and greens

233

An anxious e'e I never throws
Behint my lug, or by my nose ;
I jouk beneath Misfortune's blows
          As weel's I may ;
Sworn foe to Sorrow, Care, and Prose,
          I rhyme away.

O ye douce folk, that live by rule,
Grave, tideless-blooded, calm and cool,
Compar'd wi' you—O fool ! fool ! fool !
          How much unlike !
Your hearts are just a standing pool,
          Your lives, a dyke !

Nae hair-brain'd, sentimental traces
In your unletter'd, nameless faces !
In *arioso* trills and graces
          Ye never stray,
But *gravissimo*, solemn basses
          Ye hum away.

Ye are sae *grave*, nae doubt ye're *wise* ;
Nae ferly tho' ye do despise
The hairum-scairum, ram-stam boys,
          The rattlin squad :
I see you upward cast your eyes—
          —Ye ken the road.—

Whilst I—but I shall haud me there—
Wi' you I'll scarce gang *ony where*—
Then, *Jamie*, I shall say nae mair,

    lug] ear   jouk] duck   ferly] wonder   haud] hold

> But quat my sang.
> Content wi' *You* to mak a pair,
> Whare'er I gang.

quat] quit

The Cotter's Saturday Night

NOVEMBER chill blaws loud wi' angry sugh ;
  The short'ning winter-day is near a close ;
The miry beasts retreating frae the pleugh ;
  The black'ning trains o' craws to their repose :
The toil-worn *Cotter* frae his labour goes,
  This night his weekly moil is at an end,
Collects his spades, his mattocks, and his hoes,
  Hoping the *morn* in ease and rest to spend,
And weary, o'er the moor, his course does hameward
    bend.

At length his lonely Cot appears in view,
  Beneath the shelter of an aged tree ;
Th' expectant *wee-things*, toddlin, stacher through
  To meet their Dad, wi' flichterin noise an' glee.
His wee bit ingle, blinkin bonnily,
  His clean hearth-stane, his thriftie *Wifie's* smile,
The lisping infant prattling on his knee,
  Does a' his weary carking cares beguile,
An' makes him quite forget his labor an' his toil.

  sugh] sough, noise of wind   stacher] stagger   flichterin]
fluttering

Belyve the elder bairns come drapping in,
　　At service out, amang the Farmers roun' ;
Some ca' the pleugh, some herd, some tentie rin
　　A cannie errand to a neebor town :
Their eldest hope, their *Jenny*, woman grown,
　　In youthfu' bloom, Love sparkling in her e'e,
Comes hame, perhaps, to shew a braw new gown,
　　Or deposite her sair-won penny-fee,
To help her Parents dear, if they in hardship be.

Wi' joy unfeign'd brothers and sisters meet,
　　An' each for other's weelfare kindly speirs :
The social hours, swift-wing'd, unnotic'd fleet ;
　　Each tells the uncos that he sees or hears ;
The Parents, partial, eye their hopeful years ;
　　Anticipation forward points the view.
The *Mother*, wi' her needle an' her sheers,
　　Gars auld claes look amaist as weel's the new ;
The *Father* mixes a' wi' admonition due.

Their Master's an' their Mistress's command,
　　The younkers a' are warned to obey ;
An' mind their labours wi' an eydent hand,
　　An' ne'er, tho' out o' sight, to jauk or play ;
' An' O ! be sure to fear the Lord alway !
　　' An' mind your *duty*, duely, morn an' night !
' Lest in temptation's path ye gang astray,
　　' Implore his counsel and assisting might :
' They never sought in vain that sought the Lord
　　aright.'

belyve] by and by　　ca'] drive　　tentie] heedful
sair] sore, hard　　speirs] asks　　uncos] strange things
gars] makes　　claes] clothes　　eydent] diligent　　jauk] trifle
236

But hark ! a rap comes gently to the door ;
  Jenny, wha kens the meaning o' the same,
Tells how a neebor lad cam o'er the moor,
  To do some errands, and convoy her hame.
The wily mother sees the conscious flame
  Sparkle in *Jenny's* e'e, and flush her cheek ;
With heart-struck anxious care, enquires his name,
  While *Jenny* hafflins is afraid to speak ;
Weel pleas'd the Mother hears, it's nae wild, worthless
    Rake.

Wi' kindly welcome *Jenny* brings him ben ;
  A strappan youth ; he takes the Mother's eye ;
Blythe *Jenny* sees the visit's no ill ta'en ;
  The Father cracks of horses, pleughs, and kye.
The Youngster's artless heart o'erflows wi' joy,
  But blate and laithfu', scarce can weel behave ;
The Mother, wi' a woman's wiles, can spy
  What makes the youth sae bashfu' an' sae grave ;
Weel pleas'd to think her *bairn's* respected like the
    lave.

O happy love ! where love like this is found !
  O heart-felt raptures ! bliss beyond compare !
I've paced much this weary, mortal round,
  And sage *Experience* bids me this declare—
' If Heav'n a draught of heav'nly pleasure spare,
  ' One cordial in this melancholy Vale,
' 'Tis when a youthful, loving, modest Pair,

hafflins] half   kye] cows, cattle   blate] shy, bashful
    laithfu'] loathful   the lave] the rest

'In other's arms breathe out the tender tale,
'Beneath the milk-white thorn that scents the ev'ning
gale.'

    ·   ·   ·   ·   ·

But now the Supper crowns their simple board,
    The healsome *Parritch*, chief o' *Scotia's* food :
The soupe their only *Hawkie* does afford,
    That 'yont the hallan snugly chows her cood :
The dame brings forth in complimental mood,
    To grace the lad, her weel-hain'd kebbuck, fell,
An' aft he's prest, an' aft he ca's it guid ;
    The frugal Wifie, garrulous, will tell,
How 'twas a towmond auld, sin' Lint was i' the bell.

The cheerfu' Supper done, wi' serious face,
    They, round the ingle, form a circle wide ;
The sire turns-o'er, wi' patriarchal grace,
    The big *ha'-Bible*, ance his Father's pride :
His bonnet rev'rently is laid aside,
    His lyart haffets wearing thin an' bare ;
Those strains that once did sweet in Zion glide,
    He wales a portion with judicious care ;
And ' *Let us worship* GOD ! ' he says, with solemn air.

They chant their artless notes in simple guise ;
    They tune their hearts, by far the noblest aim :
Perhaps *Dundee's* wild warbling measures rise,
    Or plaintive *Martyrs*, worthy of the name ;

healsome] wholesome   hawkie] a white-faced cow   'yont]
beyond   hallan] partition wall   hain'd] saved   kebbuck]
cheese   fell] sharp   towmond] twelve-month   lint i' the bell]
flax in flower   lyart] grey   haffets] temples, cheeks   wales]
chooses

Or noble *Elgin* beets the heav'n-ward flame,
  The sweetest far of *Scotia*'s holy lays :
Compar'd with these, Italian trills are tame ;
  The tickl'd ears no heart-felt raptures raise ;
Nae unison hae they with our Creator's praise.

     .   .   .   .   .

Then homeward all take off their sev'ral way ;
  The youngling Cottagers retire to rest :
The Parent pair their *secret homage* pay,
  And proffer up to Heav'n the warm request,
That *He* who stills the raven's clam'rous nest,
  And decks the lily fair in flow'ry pride,
Would in the way His Wisdom sees the best,
  For them and for their little ones provide ;
But chiefly, in their hearts with *Grace divine* preside.

POEMS.

beets] adds fuel to

To a Mouse

*On turning her up in her nest with the plough,
November 1785*

  Wee, sleekit, cowrin, tim'rous beastie,
O, what a panic's in thy breastie !
Thou need na start awa sae hasty,
        Wi' bickering brattle !
I wad be laith to rin an' chase thee,
        Wi' murd'ring *pattle !*

brattle] scamper   pattle] plough-staff

I'm truly sorry Man's dominion
Has broken Nature's social union,
An' justifies that ill opinion
   Which makes thee startle
At me, thy poor, earth-born companion,
   An' *fellow-mortal!*

 I doubt na, whyles, but thou may thieve;
What then? poor beastie, thou maun live!
A *daimen icker* in a *thrave*
   'S a sma' request.
I'll get a blessin wi' the lave,
   And never miss't!

 Thy wee bit *housie*, too, in ruin!
Its silly wa's the win's are strewin!
An' naething, now, to big a new ane,
   O' foggage green!
An' bleak December's winds ensuin,
   Baith snell and keen!

 Thou saw the fields laid bare an' waste,
An' weary Winter comin fast,
An' cozie here, beneath the blast,
   Thou thought to dwell,
Till crash! the cruel *coulter* past
   Out thro' thy cell.

 That wee bit heap o' leaves an' stibble,
Has cost thee mony a weary nibble!
Now thou's turn'd out, for a' thy trouble,

daimen] odd   icker] ear of corn thrave] twenty-four
sheaves big] build foggage] coarse grass snell] biting

But house or hald,
To thole the Winter's sleety dribble,
An' cranreuch cauld !

But, Mousie, thou art no thy lane,
In proving *foresight* may be vain :
The best-laid schemes o' *Mice* an' *Men*,
Gang aft a-gley,
An' lea'e us nought but grief and pain,
For promis'd joy.

Still thou art blest, compar'd wi' *me !*
The present only toucheth thee :
But, Och ! I backward cast my e'e,
On prospects drear !
An' forward, tho' I canna *see*,
I *guess* an' *fear !*

POEMS

but] without   thole] endure   cranreuch] hoar-frost
thy lane] by thyself   a-gley] askew

Epistle to Davie, A Brother Poet

WHILE winds frae aff *Ben-Lomond* blaw,
And bar the doors wi' driving snaw,
And hing us owre the ingle,
I set me down, to pass the time,
And spin a verse or twa o' rhyme,
In hamely westlin jingle.

hing] hang   westlin] westland

While frosty winds blaw in the drift,
　　Ben to the chimla lug,
I grudge a wee the Great folk's gift,
　　That live sae bien an' snug :
　　　　I tent less, and want less
　　　　　Their roomy fire-side ;
　　　　But hanker and canker,
　　　　　To see their cursed pride.

It's hardly in a body's pow'r,
To keep, at times, frae being sour,
　　To see how things are shar'd ;
How best o' chiels are whiles in want,
While coofs on countless thousands rant,
　　And ken na how to wair't :
But *Davie*, lad, ne'er fash your head,
　　Tho' we hae little gear,
We're fit to win our daily bread,
　　As lang's we're hale and fier :
　　　　' Mair spier na, nor fear na',
　　　　　Auld age ne'er mind a feg,
　　　　The last o't, the warst o't,
　　　　　Is only but to beg.

To lie in kilns and barns at e'en,
When banes are craz'd, and bluid is thin,
　　Is, doubtless, great distress !
Yet then content could make us blest ;

ben . . . lug] in to the chimney corner　　bien] comfortabl
tent] care for　　chiels] fellows　　coofs] blockheads　　rant
roister　　wair] spend　　fash] trouble　　fier] healthy　　mai
spier na] more ask not (quotation from Ramsay)　　feg] f

Ev'n then, sometimes we'd snatch a taste
　Of truest happiness.
The honest heart that's free frae a'
　Intended fraud or guile,
However Fortune kick the ba',
　　Has ay some cause to smile,
　　　And mind still, you'll find still,
　　　　A comfort this nae sma';
　　　Nae mair then, we'll care then,
　　　　Nae farther can we fa'.

What tho', like Commoners of air,
We wander out, we know not where,
　But either house or hal'?
Yet Nature's charms, the hills and woods,
The sweeping vales, and foaming floods,
　Are free alike to all.
In days when Daisies deck the ground,
　And Blackbirds whistle clear,
With honest joy our hearts will bound,
　To see the coming year :
　　On braes when we please, then,
　　　We'll sit and sowth a tune ;
　　Syne *rhyme* till't, we'll time till't,
　　　And sing't when we hae done.

It's no in titles nor in rank ;
It's no in wealth like Lon'on Bank,
　To purchase peace and rest ;
It's no in makin muckle *mair* :

sowth] hum, whistle softly　　syne] then　　till't] to it
　　　　muckle mair] much more

It's no in books ; it's no in lear,
  To make us truly blest :
If Happiness hae not her seat
  And centre in the breast,
We may be wise, or rich, or great,
  But never can be blest :
    Nae treasures, nor pleasures,
      Could make us happy lang ;
    The *heart* ay's the part ay,
      That makes us right or wrang.

POEMS.

lear] lore, learning

The Farewell

It was a' for our rightfu' king
  We left fair Scotland's strand ;
It was a' for our rightfu' king
  We e'er saw Irish land,
    My dear,
  We e'er saw Irish land.

Now a' is done that man can do,
  And a' is done in vain ;
My love and native land farewell,
  For I maun cross the main,
    My dear,
  For I maun cross the main.

244

He turned him right and round about
   Upon the Irish shore ;
And gae his bridle-reins a shake,
   With Adieu for evermore,
         My dear,
   Adieu for evermore.

The sodger frae the wars returns,
   The sailor frae the main ;
But I hae parted frae my love,
   Never to meet again,
         My dear,
   Never to meet again.

When day is gane, and night is come,
   And a' folks bound to sleep ;
I think on him that's far awa',
   The lee-lang night, and weep,
         My dear,
   The lee-lang night, and weep.

Index of Authors

INDEX OF AUTHORS

INDEX OF AUTHORS

INDEX OF AUTHORS

Index of Titles

INDEX OF TITLES

INDEX OF TITLES

INDEX OF TITLES

INDEX OF TITLES

Printed in Great Britain by Butler & Tanner Ltd., Frome and London

THE PHOENIX LIBRARY

Pocket size, 3s. 6d. net per volume.

16. ESSAYS OF A BIOLOGIST *by* JULIAN HUXLEY.

By the Professor of Zoology at King's College, the University of London. 'It is by a maker of new biological knowledge who is also a scholar and a poet.' *Prof. J. Arthur Thomson* in *The Observer*.

17. PLAYS *by* RICHARD HUGHES.

Previously issued by another publisher. Revised and reset. The contents are: 'The Sisters Tragedy,' 'A Comedy of Good and Evil' (of which *Mr. Bernard Shaw* wrote, 'Anyone who can't enjoy all this must be an idiot'), 'The Man Born to be Hanged' and 'Danger.'

18. LIMBO *by* ALDOUS HUXLEY.

Six stories ('Farcical History of Richard Greenow,' 'Happily Ever After,' 'Eupompus Gave Splendour to Art by Numbers,' 'Cynthia,' 'The Bookshop,' and 'The Death of Lully') and a one-act play, 'Happy Families.'

19. SECOND PLAYS *by* A. A. MILNE.

Containing: 'Mr. Pim Passes By'; 'The Romantic Age'; 'Make Believe'; 'The Camberley Triangle' and 'The Stepmother.'

20. THE RIGHT PLACE *by* C. E. MONTAGUE.

A book on holiday travel, of which *The Sunday Times* said: 'A tonic to the mind and spirit of man, his book cannot be overpraised.'

21. THE SAILOR'S RETURN *by* DAVID GARNETT.

Mr. Garnett's third story, longer than either *Lady Into Fox* or *A Man in the Zoo*, one which was hailed by *The Empire Review* as 'a masterpiece.'

22. MORTAL COILS *by* ALDOUS HUXLEY.

Short stories, containing 'The Gioconda Smile,' 'Permutations among the Nightingales,' 'The Tillotson Banquet,' 'Green Tunnels,' and 'Nuns at Luncheon.'

23. MR. WESTON'S GOOD WINE *by* T. F. POWYS.

The first unlimited edition of Mr. Powys's longest and greatest story. 'Worthy at once to take its place among the great allegories of English literature.' *The Bookman*.

24. LOLLY WILLOWES *by* Sylvia Townsend Warner.
The witch-story hailed by *The Times Literary Supplement* as 'an object lesson in the proper way of bringing Satan into modern fiction.'

25. ON THE MARGIN *by* Aldous Huxley.
Notes and essays on such subjects as 'Centenaries,' 'The Subject-Matter of Poetry,' 'Bibliophily,' 'Nationality in Love,' 'Chaucer,' etc. 'One of the most interesting and provocative of the younger generation of English men of letters.' *The Daily Telegraph.*

26. THE GRIM SMILE OF THE FIVE TOWNS
by Arnold Bennett.
Here, as in all his Five Town stories, Mr. Bennett's humour and buoyancy are unfailing.

27. TARR *by* Wyndham Lewis.
Mr. Wyndham Lewis's novel, long out of print, is here completely revised. From reviews of the first edition: 'A book of great importance . . . because it will become a date in literature.' *The New Witness.* 'A thunderbolt.' *The Weekly Dispatch.*

28. LITTLE MEXICAN *by* Aldous Huxley.
Short stories, containing: 'Uncle Spencer,' 'Little Mexican,' 'Hubert and Minnie,' 'Fard,' 'The Portrait,' and 'Young Archimedes.' 'The opulence of Mr. Huxley's talent speaks in every page.' *The Observer.*

29. LOVE & FREINDSHIP *by* Jane Austen.
And other Early Works now first published, with an Introduction by G. K. Chesterton, who writes: 'A thing to laugh over again and again.'

30. THREE PLAYS *by* A. A. Milne.
Containing: 'The Great Broxopp'; 'The Dover Road'; 'The Truth about Blayds.'

31. THE HOUSE WITH THE ECHO *by* T. F. Powys.
'Connoisseurs of the short story should not miss this little book, for Mr. Powys has a rare mastery of the art.' *The Evening Standard.*

32. SWANN'S WAY, vol. 1, *by* Marcel Proust.
Translated by c. k. scott moncrieff. 'M. Proust is a
genius; and Mr. Scott Moncrieff has treated him like
one.' *The Nation.*

33. SWANN'S WAY, vol. 2, *by* Marcel Proust.
Translated by c. k. scott moncrieff. 'The translator . . .
faced a task of prodigious difficulty with extraordinary
success.' *The London Mercury.*

34. ESSAYS IN POPULAR SCIENCE by Julian Huxley.
'One of the few scientific books that is popular and scientific without patronising the reader.' *Cambridge Review.*

35. A SHORT HISTORY OF ENGLAND
by G. K. Chesterton.
'He is at once the most concise and fullest historian this
country has yet found.' *The Observer.*

36. TWO OR THREE GRACES *by* Aldous Huxley.
Four stories, one as long as a short novel. 'I have no
hesitation in saying that of the younger men writing
to-day, Mr. Huxley is in a class by himself.' *Ralph Straus*
in *The Bystander.*

37. HADRIAN VII *by* Fr. Rolfe ('Baron Corvo.')
A novel. 'There is no precedent for it in English
literature.' *A. J. A. Symons* in *Life and Letters.*

38. THE GENTLE ART OF COOKERY
by Mrs. C. F. Leyel *and* Miss Olga Hartley.
A really original cookery book which 'no properly in-
stituted home should be without.' *The Morning Post.*

39. ROUGH JUSTICE *by* C. E. Montague.
A novel. 'A beautiful and a terrible book. . . . A masterpiece of fiction.' *Sir Philip Gibbs* in *The Catholic Times.*

40. FOUR PLAYS *by* A. A. Milne.
Containing: 'To Have the Honour'; 'Ariadne, or
Business First'; 'Portrait of a Gentleman in Slippers';
and 'Success.'

CHATTO & WINDUS
97 & 99 St. Martin's Lane, W.C. 2